The Philosophy and Literature of Existentialism

by Wesley Barnes, Ph.D.,

Professor of English

Morehead State University

Morehead, Kentucky

Barron's Educational Series, Inc.,

Woodbury, New York.

Contents

Preface

The purpose of this book is to give both pleasure and information through revealing the nature of existentialism, a philosophy of life primarily literary in effect. Inherent in the purpose is the point of view of the author. That viewpoint is essentially descriptive. There are no emotive overtones or undertones in defense of the existential position, or in support of the thesis. That there is an existential position and movement is verifiable through philosophical, psychological, sociological, and literary phenomena.

While this book deals primarily with the philosopher, the psychologist, and the literary figure, the existential movement has its being and operation in our current society. Our contemporary films, plays, and newspapers carry the movement and are carried by the thesis of the existing individual who strives for identity and meaning solely in and through his own terms.

The alienation, isolation, and rejection that accompany the individual who must thrust aside the social and moral claims of society as such are never absent from our mass communication. Never in man's history have there been such strong feeling and belief that the external world of things, ideas, and people are absurd beyond belief, and beyond endurance. Such TV programs as "Run For Your Life" and "The Fugitive" are uniquely typical of the existential position. If the individual does not run, his life, in the total sense of living, is lost, according to current programs aired over the networks. That this text does not detail the current programs through a discussion of them specifically springs from the twin demands of good manners and good judgment.

Historically, critics of the modern scene avoid specific references to movements and their vehicles because of being too close in time and place to them. Good manners demand that the current writers have the benefit of being viewed from a perspective far enough removed temporally and spatially to see the movements in relationship to the total number of movements in a society at a given time. Good judgment demands that the critic has sufficient distance in time and space and that he should also have allowed enough time to discover the strength of the movement over some few years. Until recently, few writers were considered seriously until their death, or until they had shown that through age or waning of inspiration they had nothing more to say, or until their thesis or slant had reached fruition. Some writers lived long enough and wrote enough to have themselves considered while still writing. Among these individuals we can number such figures as Frost, Yeats, and Hardy.

With improvement in communication, with the advantages of the speed of modern publication, with the increasing ability to bring the author and his movements to the attention of both critic and laymen in a relatively short time, modern criticism shows a trend toward considering writers while they are still writing creatively.

However, there is a limit that caution imposes, and that limit is reached in the matter of today's day by day presentations over television, radio, and screen. Thus, many most recent existential works are not discussed. We can close this part of the prefatory remarks by indicating that the "beatniks," modern adolescent dancing, and the "hippies" are each and altogether manifestations of some aspects of the existential movement. In the author's purpose, then, there are both explicit and implicit invitations to the reader to take the principles detailed and to apply them to the modern milieu of books, events, people, and new social movements.

The audience for this book has ranged, can range, and should range from the student in a formal educational situation to the layman reading at home for both pleasure and information. The material in this text has been "tried out" on students ranging from Grade Eleven through students on college or university levels, students on both undergraduate and graduate levels. There are no terms stated with such complexity as to make understanding difficult for a perceptive student or person within the areas cited above.

When we come to specific purposes, central to these are the views that existentialism should be seen as mainly literary and psychological in tone and operation, that existentialism and naturalism are easily confused unless there is more than a superficial view taken of each, and that the same observation is also true of romanticism and existentialism. From a specific educational point of view the purpose is to furnish the reader with principles which he can apply to the literary, psychological, sociological, and ethical and religious experiences, both personal and educational, that he encounters each day. Inherent in the general purpose and specific purposes are, of course, the nature and the scope of this book.

The book discriminates among different views of life—literary and otherwise—with explanatory and illustrative material. We first define each view of life through finding the unique qualities which distinguish that view. Then the procedure is that of enumerating the characteristics of each principal philosophical position. The prominent exponents of each main position are discussed and their general and specific positions set forth. The first part of the book gives an introduction, and a necessary one, from the viewpoint of defining existentialism. The very process of reaching a definition, the inductive one, reveals the uniqueness of the existential position. The reader will see that the total definition is reached through indicating that unique quality in existentialism denied other views of life, and through "defining" in a series of steps which include semantics, history, psychology, and religion, among other philosophical areas of inquiry. In each case the uniqueness takes the form of revealing that the existentialist denies all objective reality in each area of inquiry so as to make the existing individual complete within himself.

The book is presented from the point of view of a teacher and scholar who has had much theoretical and practical experience in literature, psychology, and philosophy. The philosophical treatment is not rigorous. The treatment could not be rigorous because, in the sense of the formal philosophical methods, existentialism turns out to be a complete failure.

Implicitly, at least, the reader will see that the failure of existentialism to meet the logical consistency required in philosophical thought and inquiry becomes the very strength of existentialism. Its failure, in the philosophical sense, stems not from its being "right" or "wrong" from intellectual or moral standards. Its failure is one of language, as will be shown.

Yet, because language must stem from the behavior of the individual, existentialism's failure, ultimately, must be traced to the phenomenon of man's personality. History—language-wise, at least—reveals that each man has always acknowledged external standards as making claims upon him. The existentialist denies such claims and denies external reality, but he is born into a common language that will not permit him to articulate his position.

The overall position taken in this book is that existentialism, as an operational view of life and literature, is both powerful and pervasive. Its force stems from its lyrical appeal in that thinking with feeling is never stronger than when articulated through the individual. The extreme sense of self that is so unique to the existentialist makes for the most intense—and painful—fusion of thinking with feeling about the self as existing in the light of the self, only.

There is no question that today's individual is striving desperately for self-consciousness of the self as one existence that is vitally important. The continual round of wars, the succession of group encounters in the fields of economics and politics, and the bloody intermittent racial conflicts, together with other group struggles, have driven the individual to desperate straits. He will deny all certitude outside himself on the grounds that he can do no worse for himself than is done by society, or he will adopt a view of life that will accept the agony, despair, alienation, and isolation that will come from creating a position that can yield only a consciousness of the single existing individual. The existentialist asserts that to be free is to choose one's own living and dying. He may as well die on his own terms as on the terms of others. But the existentialist cannot choose such a freedom without also buying, at the same time, a brand of slavery. By adopting such a philosophy the existentialist must find himself condemned to live without either the horror or the glory that is the heritage and the order of life—society.

Since man by nature desires to know, this book is an attempt to reveal one of the creeds by which some bold but desperate men live.

WESLEY BARNES

Chapter 1

Is Existentialism Definable?

Problems of Definition

Words do not have meanings: they carry meanings. A word, as such, has no meaning, but each word, in context, carries at least one meaning, and, usually, multiple meanings. The word is not the thing, idea, event, person, or institution, but is that which stands for the thing, idea, event, person, or institution. Such must be the case with existentialism, a word. Existentialism, then, must carry a range of meanings, and the term will be defined, for this book, in the light of what a word can do—no more, or no less.

To define is to be logical, and to be logical, sometimes a human attribute, is to use some method of analysis. We must keep in mind, however, that definition is a process, one which leads to communication. Without going too deeply into this thorny matter of communication, the thesis on that score is that "communication" has taken place when the range of meanings inherent in the writer or speaker is understood by the reader or listener in the same range of meanings. What is important at this point is the realization that understanding does not equate with agreement. From a linguistical point of view—the only truly profitable one—the process of discovery as to the nature of existentialism should be inductive, not deductive. Nevertheless, we shall commence with a definition of existentialism from the point of view of uniqueness.

There are many dictionary definitions of "existentialism"; each carries some degree of truth. These will not be discussed, nor will they be analyzed since that process would involve several volumes. However, central to each definition is the assertion that existentialism is a theory or statement about the nature of man's existence. There is entire agreement about that point. Errors come from accompanying statements that scientific or idealistic approaches are not adequate in defining or understanding existentialism.

Let us understand clearly that no theory of any kind of human existence can be defined in terms solely those of a scientific or idealistic process. Definition, as must be true of any other process, must be a matter of total personality. As such, existentialism must involve the viewpoints of thinking, feeling, and sensing. Second, existentialism, overall, and existentialism, as reflected specifically in any behavioral account of its operation—is subject to the scientific detection of its operation through any one of several modern psychological approaches. Different emotive states carry their principles into operation through certain unique linguistic structures, both macroscopic and miscroscopic. Those operating in an "existential way" can be identified as uniquely different from the other theories of human existence.

Existentialism is one of a limited number of views of man's nature, central to which is his existence. The other views are that man's nature is one that falls into one of the following categories: an operational balance among the elements of thought, feeling, and sensation—classicism, an imbalance weighted in favor of the world of volitions (feeling, emotions, and will) over the world of mind and senses—romanticism, an imbalance among the categories of head, heart, and hand in favor of thought—rationalism; an imbalance resulting from choosing the world of materiality—the world of the senses and things, over the claims of spirit and thought—naturalism.

Then existentialism is a view of human existence, and, as such, finds itself in the class with classicism, romanticism, rationalism, and naturalism. Obviously, for each individual, the meanings of each view must be carried by words which have ranges of meaning. If we can find one of the views which differs from all other views in accepting a range of meaning, then the view can be defined at least from a semantic point of view. Whether one is a romanticist, a rationalist, a classicist, or one in the grim hold of naturalism, he accepts words describing each as holding the same range of meanings for all views, even including that of existentialism. He accepts the range of meanings describing each one, although he selects from the range according to his unique viewpoint. However, since the existentialist denies that he can be bound to the external control of any range of meanings, including those of words, he can be defined as uniquely different from his *philosophers*. Here, the definition, and an effective one, is on semantical grounds. He creates his own range of meanings of words; if they approach those used in the other philosophies of man's existence, they do so only accidentally. The existentialist deliberately—and unconsciously sometimes—rejects traditional ranges of meaning in his own language environment. Quite often he does so through using the words in an opposite sense. We could rest on this linguistic view, and do so safely, did we so desire. However, we can also define existentialism in the light of a historical uniqueness.

Denial of External Historical Sense

As with the question of words, the romantic, the classical, the rationalistic, and the naturalistic theorists have emphasized one quality of personality over others, but they have accepted the historical existence and nature of each as a fact. The existentialist denies any external historical sense. He is personally and objectively without history. Thus, we could assert that existentialism is that view of the nature of man which asserts that there is no objective oral or written history of past natural and human events which exists or which he must consider. Since all other views of man's existence accept a concept of "history" as an external force, each existentialist has another unique quality which should define him, as an existentialist.

Were the essentialist* to define his experience in terms of being able to view the flow of thoughts, emotions, and sensory materials in the mind at any one cross-section of time, he would hold, according to his own brand of personal, formal, and literary philosophy, that the flow could be objectively measured as that primarily of concepts (the rationalist), emotions (the romanticist), perceptual stuffs (the believer in naturalism), and a "proper" blend of each for that time and place (the classicist). The existentialist, in his experience with what we would call "phenomonology," would be conscious of a flowing of experience, which consciously would be restricted en-

---

* (The essentialist is one of the following: rationalist, romanticist, believer in naturalism or classicist.)

tirely to that of the self. The flow would be proof of his own existing. The flowing of experience in terms of thoughts, emotions, and percepts, would not be that which could be measured as apart from or distinct from himself. The flow would not measure himself against any objective standard of thinking, feeling, and sensing that could be equated against any standard other than his own. Again, for the existentialist, the flowing of experience, as being known by himself at any one time, could not be measured against his consciousness of his own mind at any other time. Thus, the existentialist, then, can be defined, uniquely, in terms of his theory of the mind as stated by the non-existentialist.

We must realize that the non-existentialist must do the defining since the phenomenon of definition would be entirely alien to the existentialist. He would see defining as the fatal process of setting up standards which he would have to consider, admit, deny, or modify.

When we come to physical nature and to its laws, again we find the same general reaction: the essentialist pins himself to a consideration of the external world and to his internal views of this world in the light of his basic and measurable philosophy. The rationalist considers the world of nature and its laws as intellectually verifiable. The romanticist considers the external world and its laws in terms of being either inferior to the world of imagination or as in opposition to the world of intuition. The believer in naturalism considers the world of nature and its laws as the one total controlling force, a force against which man, in error, rebels, or a force which man, through wise decision, accepts. The classical point of view considers the world of nature and the world of man as necessary in cooperation and conflict in the sense of enabling man's tripartite* nature to develop in correct proportions. But, the existential view is uniquely different. The other views accept outside forces as existing apart from themselves.

Flow of Consciousness

The existential point of view is that all forms of experience, whether they be directly from the external world of physical nature and its laws or not, have no value other than being just one stimulus or set of stimuli which provide a flow of consciousness through which the existentialist becomes conscious of his own existing. This existing is known through willing, choosing, suffering, agonizing, despairing, and being free.

When we adhere through our total commitments in terms of personality to forces outside ourselves, we are in the field of religion. The religion of the rationalists is that of reason, that of the romanticists is one of feeling, that of the believer in naturalism is that of external nature as god or God, and that of the classicist is a harmonious expression of mind, body, and spirit in response to or interaction with external forces. The existentialist has for his religion his consciousness of experiencing. This continuous but varied consciousness of existing becomes a deification of his feeling and sensing through choosing, willing, deciding, and through all other forms of "ing" where these forms lead to process and not to a conclusion. (The existentialist adopts the intransitive view of life "I am kicking." He refutes the transitive view of life: "I am kicking the ball.") The existentialist, then, does not have a

---

* Personality, throughout this book, is considered as being the interacting elements of thinking, feeling, and sensing as revealed in human behavior.

purpose, but, if he could choose his own world of language, he would declare he is "purposing."

The Contradictions of Existentialism

We will be somewhat ahead of the game if we can grasp the critical point that one drawback of the existential position is that the individual who is an existentialist is hampered because he is born into our language which admits of other sentence patterns than the intransitive statement. "Purposing" is not in our dictionary, but for his own dictionary, could he but have one, such words would be indispensable. In order to create his own world of process he must use terms which express process—such as "going," "purposing," and "phenomonalizing," among many others.

Whether our friend the existentialist seems to have a thesis worthy of urging or not, we would have to admit that his being forced to urge his side of the case in the form of language which cannot express his position is a bitter irony. One argument, of course, is that human experience, working through many languages over many times, does not, from this historical point of view, admit such a philosophy as his. That is, since language must be the product of human behavior, no human behavior we have known has demanded the kind of language the existentialist needs. In order, therefore, for the existentialist to live with his position, he must declare any outside world of experience as uncertain and without purpose. He must deny, at all cost, the direct object, when such an object can be other than his own consciousness of his own existing. We can see why, perhaps, he looks to the flow of his own mind as proof of existing, and denies, utterly, outside reality. (The outside reality he fears more than any other is that essential philosophy of naturalism.) The existentialist is accused of being contradictory. We would be fairer were we to say that in our own definition—since he will not define—we accuse him of being contradictory in denying absolutes in order to make his own existing a God, or an absolute.

However, we are in no position to labor this point of being contradictory. The believer in rationalism contradicts the facts of total personality, as do the romanticist, the believer in naturalism, and the classicist. To make mind, will, body, or "proportion" themselves absolutes, the essentialist contradicts the facts of existing, one of which is consciousness of the self and the outside world.

Using our own words, and not his "wording," we define for him his own existing—a rather dangerous and unreliable act. However, we have no other recourse. We must be forced to admit that even when we labor our position as essentialists as one of being totally objective, we are in error. To objectify the truth of reasons, as rational, for example, we become subjective because we rule out the other "isms." We are now at the point of realizing that the mere process of definition is in itself subjective in terms of that which is not defined. The more carefully we define, the more we exclude more outside reality.

While, as we shall see later, existentialism is not philosophically defensible, we dare not condemn existentialism on the grounds of subjectivity and then urge such a subjectivity as the grounds for differentiation between the essential and the existentialistic. Again, as has been indicated earlier, existentialism, as a philosophy, must fail on the grounds that it supports its thesis by essentialistic methods. These methods are both matters of thinking, feeling, and sensing, but they also involve linguistical problems, as we have seen. We cannot, then, define existentialism in the forms found in our current dictionaries. We have been defining inductively. We reach the position where we must give a condensed catch-all definition. We must admit, of course, our linguistical difficulties. This admission must come from our knowledge that our language has been developed along the lines of explaining ends or accomplishments rather than along the line of "processing."

Existentialism "Defined"

Existentialism is the view of life which focuses on "a man" and, in so doing, denies that any man is to be measured or equated against any class called "man" in any sense of experience. Since "man" traditionally is classified in terms of his mind, body, and will against the framework of an external world, the existential position denies, utterly, the certainty of any external world, as object, and denies, utterly, the assertion that any rule—physical, emotive, or intellectual—is valid in relation to the single individual. Existentialism, then, is the consciousness of a man that he is existing in terms of his own flowing of experience, a flow which he can know, feel, and sense only within himself. From this definition we can derive, as has been done, the concepts of freedom on one hand and of slavery on the other hand. The existentialist, *a* man, is free to choose because there are no objective standards to inhibit or constrain his choice. He must choose, since his flowing of experience, as discoverable within himself—through his mental flow of experience—is such as to demand that he select one alternative from many. Of course, these alternatives must come from his own consciousness of his consciousness. (Here we have a philosophical problem.)

His freedom must be saturated with the snarl-like emotions of agony, despair, disgust, and the feeling of being absurd. Such must be the case because he can never use the words "I have made the right decision." There are no standards against which he can equate that which is "right." Having declared all consciousness of a thing other than his existing self as non-certain and without purpose, he can never have any object "out there" in what we call the real world of people, ideas, and things. His freedom consists in "choosing." However, he is also enslaved because he is free to choose or not to choose. But he is never free not to choose or not to choose not to choose. All that follows, then, in this relatively short treatment of existentialism, will demonstrate concretely the developments of the existential position in philosophy, psychology, and literature. The point made in the "Preface" to this book is that existentialism has its impact, validity, and concern in the literary sense. In fact, the main reason for considering philosophy and psychology in this treatment of existentialism is that the philosophers and psychologists treating of the subject are far more literary than philosophical. Since literature is thinking with feeling about experience, all writers thinking with feeling find themselves in the literary purview. The most effective philosophical statements concerning this existential view of life, and of the single man, are those made by such figures as Dostoevsky, Pascal, Nietzsche, Heidegger, Sartre, and Buber, among others.

We approach existentialism specifically and fruitfully with the belief that understanding will come through an examination of the philosophical, scientific, psychological, and religious theories of the past—and the expression of these theories in writing: through an indication of the reasons why traditional philosophies and the literature that has often been their vehicle no longer satisfied; through an analysis of the evolution of existentialism and its three discernibly different modern developments; through the capitulation of the tenets of existentialism and comparison of those tenets with the attitudes of other literary philosophies; finally, through a description of the views of all representative existential philosophers, or literary exponents, with the emphasis upon their writings.

Chapter 2

■

A Man as Opposed to Man

Traditional Philosophy and Man's Problems

For all men and in all of their philosophies, there has been a consciousness of man and his problems.

The Renaissance thinkers—and the Reformation thinkers—were certain that they knew that there were problems connected with the vertical world and with the horizontal world. For the man of the Reformation, many of the problems would disappear could the spirit of the Renaissance be quelled or muted. For the Renaissance individual, the problems could be solved by a matter of primacy: man and the horizontal world then man and God next. There was a little matter of mind and body to be resolved before the preparation for eternity. The conflict—and the cooperation, at times—between the Renaissance and the Counter-Renaissance was waged primarily in intellectual terms. Nevertheless, each side viewed its position and its results with some optimism, however well-founded or ill-founded. The intellect, having savored its strength and having found its tastes to its liking, forged to the fore in the eighteenth century.

In the Age of Rationalism, or Neoclassicism, or the Augustan Age, or the Age of Newton, man believed that the rational powers could answer all questions: the questions of the laws of a suddenly-discovered horizontal world, the questions of deism, the questions of ethics, and the questions of economics, sociology, and politics. Man placed his faith in the rationale of the laws of mathematics. He was confident in man's own anthropocentrism, his superiority through being a man of intellect—or reason.

As man moved along toward the nineteenth century, he felt that the will, the volitions, and the emotive power of man needed expression. This expression was considered so powerful as to be almost divine in its imaginative range.

The romanticist, who now decided to place the mind and the body under control of the will, agreed that there were problems. However, through using the imagination, the problems could be solved. First, in a religious sense, the problems could be solved through faith and man's emotional range. In every other sense, the individual could create a world, an objective world, without the same problems. This world could be created through the imaginative range of great poets—such as Shelley and Coleridge, for example. This world could be ignored because the imagination could create a better world in its own terms. Or the problems of the world could be ignored as beneath the notice of the romanticist. However, the romanticist, deprecating the value of mind and senses, did not reject them. He did not reject materiality completely, only for its own sake. He used materiality to explain an imaginative world without materiality.

The romanticist often seemed quite disillusioned with the world as material and intellectual. The fact that he often ignored problems did not mean that he admitted that they could not be solved. Although there were many varieties of romanticism, including escapism, no romanticist admitted lack of competence. He did assert that the world that existed in the light of the problems he found was not worth saving—Shelley. But the Victorian, his successor, held no such romantic confidence.

From the 1840's on, the Victorian temperament—by no means a cowardly one—found problems of many kinds. The majority of the problems stemmed from man's pursuit of material well-being and from his political and social institutions raised in support of that well-advertised pursuit—happiness. Added to the Victorian's woes over materialism came the scientific determinism inherent in Darwinian theory and its apparent and real threats to both established church and freethinker churches. The Victorians had worlds of problems, and they enjoyed every problem. No other age in history has been filled with so many and so varied lamentations, lamentations in which Tennyson, Arnold, Kipling, Hardy, and lesser souls participated. The significant point is that the Victorians were honest in confronting the problems—even if they sometimes seemed to seek them out. Furthermore, and most significant, they were quite certain that the problems could not really be solved. However, each Victorian seemed willing to try to give a solution to the problems—even if the solutions were sweetness and light, positivism, neo-symbolism, free high schools, suffrage, or "all's right with the world." At the turn of the century, "realism" as method was beginning to be palmed off as philosophy.

The "realists" commenced the attack on traditional attitudes by agreeing that problems could not be solved, but they could be revealed, and revealed simply for their own sakes. At first, the confession that the people of the time could not solve the problems, but could highlight them, was dishonest. The dishonesty came in the selectivity of the realistic details. What we had was not a philosophy, but a method, a form. Instead of stating traditional conflict in the light of which there was a solution, even if temporary, the "realists" (James and Howell, for example) revealed crisis, but not conflict.

However, science and the world of man and his pursuit of materialism were not long inclined to permit this dishonesty to continue. Naturalism struck and struck savagely. Gissing, Hardy, Lawrence, Housman, London, Norris (and, earlier, Flaubert and Zola), Dreiser, Steinbeck, and Hemingway revealed the power of an all-encompassing nature; they fled to art for its own expression, quite avoiding any moral or spiritual—even intellectual—implications of their literary skill. They as much as stated that their sole responsibility was to show the form of nature as she exists. The only "ought" and "should" they admitted refer to the structure of the expression of the world of things as they appear and are. There has never been any question in the art of these writers that nature is supreme. Man is only an accidental expression of colliding atoms which continuously move in random fashion. Absolutes in the moral sense or in the intellectual sense have no more value than any other phenomenon, nor any more permanence. The sole god is not the atom or its constituents, but the laws of constant and random movement of the basic matter. Thus, no problems can be solved; they simply exist. Thus, what exists, does so, and does so on its own terms, no term of which is solvable through man's intellectual, spiritual, or material components of his personality. In naturalism, both spirit and mind are in matter. In rationalism, spirit and matter are controlled by mind; in romanticism, mind and materiality are at the service or disposal of the heart; in the classical tradition, mind, body, and spirit fuse in the right proportion at the right time to cope with material, intellectual, or supernatural problems.

Material Determinism

Thus, close to our own era, we have witnessed the superiority of materiality in its own atomic right—and rites. Science views naturalism intellectually. Science sees an impersonal order of constant change, an orderly change, or an orderly disorder. Science's "ought" and "should" are confined to method. Scientists have made a religion of impersonal observation. In this sense they have been truer to their religion than the nonscientist has been to his own.

Traditional religion has retreated where no retreat was demanded. It has accepted science's view of the supernatural as not proven by "ordinary or mathematical means" as meaning not capable of proof. Religion has abandoned the supernatural in favor of the "super-ethical natural." She has fought a halfhearted battle against the id, ego, and superego of Freud; finally, she has accepted the role of giving as much metaphysical proof as possible—which is little or none—to the concept that there is less misery in a group-oriented society than there is in a society of rugged individuals. To have meaningful experiences as indicated by the mutual back-slapping of other members of a society of mutual back-slappers is to have an ethical and joyful experience. Or, put another way, the misery which comes from living in a natural order that deludes us by letting us delude ourselves that we are superior to the stuff from which we sprang and to which we must assuredly return, is more endurable in a group society where the blame and praise can be equally distributed. In fact, if we work hard enough at this delusion, we can believe that as a group organism we are superior to the stuff—our mother, father, tester, and executioner—nature. Thus, from the Renaissance and through some five or six hundred years, man has managed to shed, one by one, the facets of personality—mind, spirit, and body. He has managed to dispose of his individual problems. No man can solve a world of complete material determinism.

Within the past fifty years a different approach has made itself felt in literature, psychology, psychiatry, and sociology. The traditional philosophies had beliefs and attitudes toward a reality based on a total theory of the known universe and man's place therein. In other words, each philosophy, while differing in degree, had a complete theory for all nature: the nature of man, the nature of the universe, and the nature of God. While each individual differed from all other individuals in degree of the attributes of man, each individual had each of the attributes. The individual measured himself against the totality of man as represented through his specific philosophical school of thought. This position brings us to the point of examination of *essence*.

The Nature of Essence

In biology the individual first derives its meaning from the phylum, then more specifically from the subphylum, then through class, superorder, order, down to species. Traditionally, we view man in terms of the qualities of him as man—and what differentiates him from other forms of life. The essence of man is expressed the same way. When we define a person or thing, we give certain qualities of each. Now, a cat and man have certain attributes in common; for example, each belongs to the phylum Chordata, subphylum Vertebrate, and class Mammalia. As they become compared and contrasted in greater degree, they are separable in the light of what makes a cat a cat and not a man. Thus, in defining, in stating essence, and in determining the "nature of," we state certain qualities of mind, spirit, and materiality which reach the point where the definition, nature of, and essence depend on that collection of factors that belong solely to the one, as apart from all others.

Man finds himself classified with the Primates; however, further subdivisions are made on the basis of unique qualities present in man and not in the other members of the primates. We reach the point where we define man with a list of enumerable qualities, including those which separate mankind from other forms of life. Apart from the essence he has with forms of life as a member of the same phylum, subphylum, and class, man is unique in many respects. Among these respects are the ability to build fire, to make tools, to pass intellectual judgments, to evaluate his past and present, to speculate on the supernatural, and to organize his world of experience in the categories of love, play, religion, and work. These are common qualities of the essence of that which makes up man, collectively. They define the nature and essence of man, his uniqueness. Thus what we mean by essentialism and by essence is the specific list of qualities which make man "man" and which further differentiate man from other beings, animate or inanimate.

Therefore, whether we take the synthesis of the total personality of man, as with the classical tradition, or whether we accept the partial literary philosophies of romanticism, rationalism, and naturalism, we use the traditional approach of working from the qualities of man down to the unit, let us say, of a single Martha Jones. When we say that Martha is a "good" girl, the concept of good with reference to man is already with us; we apply, as closely as we can, enough of the qualities which make up the idea of "good in man" to the specific case of our Martha.

There are three facets—and only three facets—to human personality. They are mind, body, and spirit. Traditionally, the essence of man has been that each man dealt with the world of experience—things, people, ideas, events, emotions, and institutions—in terms of a personality that agreed that what he was came directly from an essence that covered every man. So firmly did man believe in the essence of man—what made man "man"—that he established absolutes in the light of religion, love, mercy, justice, kindness, awe, and sacrifice, for example. That man is controlled by externals in the light of his educational, religious, social, and political institutions, according to his own free will, is *essentialism*. The Hebraic-Christian civilizations and the civilizations of the Hellenes were constructed on the belief that a man thinks, feels, and senses—and does so because he is of the order of man. If he emphasizes the will over mind and body, he is romantic. If he prefers mind to both will and body, he is rationalistic. If he subscribes to materiality as the great truth, his is the philosophy of naturalism. If he synthesizes all aspects of personality, he is classic—but rarely so. As an essentialist, man has subordinated two or more aspects of personality, but never to the exclusion, utterly, of each —although naturalism approaches such an exclusion.

If man rejects essentialism, he must reject naturalism, classicism, romanticism, and rationalism. If he rejects essence as prior to and before existence, he is no longer an essentialist, but an existentialist.

The Meaning of Essence

What does "essence" mean? Essence is that which distinguishes and enumerates. Essence tells what qualities each man has. However, more significantly, essence tells what distinguishes one form of life or one form of an object from another. Much difficulty is avoided if we lump together the words *nature, essence,* and *definition* and treat them as being quite synonymous for our purpose. The nature of man is "that which characterizes."

Traditionally, then, mankind is defined in the light of his unique attributes, his essence. The reader should understand this defining to be more a matter of interrelationships between what man is and what other forms of life are. Mankind carries his attribute of being able to classify to the point of distinguishing among men themselves. This distinguishing involves separating men by color, religion, profession, nationality, and intellectual ability, emotional stability, and physical attributes. Nevertheless, the critical point is that the differences among men themselves as individuals are ones of degree, not of quality.

Whatever differences men may have among themselves, they possess, collectively, that which makes them different from other phyla, classes, orders, and species. While man treats, in the traditional sense, of specific men with specific names, qualities, geographical locations, and times, he does so, always, from the viewpoint of what man is as unique. The individual is measured in the light of his unique nature. For example, of the essence of man is his conscious structuring of life as composed of drives of love, of recreation, of struggle for physical survival, and of religion. In a consistent pattern one quality of man has been his consideration of a creator, one greater than he. Man can decide to accept or reject many concepts of a first cause. In some instances, his essence has taken the direction of creating several gods, of having them in the world, outside the world, or inside and outside the world. When we consider any man in a religious context, we find him conscious of supernatural matters. Being conscious of them does not mean that he always accepts a supernatural world as real. However, since he is of man, such is his nature, his essence, that he cannot avoid supernatural considerations. Because each man, unique in his own right, is composed of all of the attributes of man proper, he can understand his fellow man. Because he is of the same attributes, he can engage in conflict as well as in cooperation, also. Each man has a religious nature.

Let us assume, for the sake of a starting point, that in all religious phenomena possible to all of mankind there are numerically one hundred units and that each of the one hundred has intensities ranging from a figure of one to fifty. Let us consider that *A* has sixty-two of the phenomena, with the lowest intensity for one as a rating of twenty-six and the highest as a rating of thirty-nine. Let us further consider that *B* has eleven of the phenomena, with the lowest having an intensity of forty-five and the highest having a value of fifty. Let us further consider that of *A*'s sixty-two religious attributes and of *B*'s eleven eight are the same! Since neither has the total number and since each has only eight in common, small wonder at the number of religions and the classifications within each main religion. Small wonder the number of disagreements and conflicts. Further note that *B* holds his attributes with more intensity than does *A*. Further consider that *C* has fifty attributes and that *D* has fifty attributes. However, *C* and *D* have only ten in common. *C* holds his with a ninety per cent intensity overall, and *D* holds his with an eighty-eight per cent intensity average. What an excellent opportunity for disagreement!

There is no question as to "right" and "wrong" here. Since no one has all the qualities or intensities possible in a one hundred per cent sense, *A, B, C,* and *D* can never understand the whole completely. Yet each is right to the extent of what he has. And each man is incomplete even when he is correct! He is conscious only of an essential part of his nature. When *A* claims that *B* is wrong because they do not agree as to the details of their supernatural entities, *A* considers his own frame of reference: neither sees the whole of man's religious reality. When *A* denies that he has any religious nature, there is, of course, the slightest chance that he could be correct—in view of the law of averages as operative over large numbers. What is more likely is that *A* is not satisfied with the kind of proof— physical, intellectual, or volitional—that is offered by others to himself, to others, or by himself to himself. There is the further possibility that he does not, consciously or subconsciously, desire to believe that he has a religious essence. Of course, this line of reasoning must be based on our discussing man and each man as a rational animal.

At any rate, if we extend this line of approach to his other essences, such as ideas, emotions, aesthetic experiences, and psychological behavior, one can see what a complex creature each man is, and how much man, overall, is complex. We are often misled into believing that the contentions between schools of thought in science, philosophy, art, music, literature, politics, sociology, and psychology reflect a disagreement as to the essence of man. That is not so. The qualities that distinguish man uniquely, those referred to as the ability to articulate to himself and others concerning the worlds of mind, spirit, and body, are constant. The problems come with regard to the agreement as to how these qualities of man react with each other and react through individual men as they meet each other in the experience called "life."

We must not plunge too deeply into philosophy as such, but we must know the concerns of philosophy. We must know them because philosophy is that which concerns all conscious and subconscious experience of mankind. The philosopher realizes that the essence of man, the nature of man, is that which is common to every man. Therefore, the philosopher does not concern himself with individuals as is the case in literature. We often err in saying that because the philosopher deals with the concept of man, rather than with the sensory, intellectual, and spiritual experience of specific people living in definite places at definite times, that he is divorced from reality. Such is not the case. He handles the greater reality because no one man can have any quality that is not in the nature, the essence, of every man.

Example of Essence

When Shakespeare's Prince Hal and Hotspur contend in Henry IV, Part I, Shakespeare is talking of two real people who at a certain time and place in English history contended over specific problems. The first problem was Hotspur's grievance; the next, his stubborn and fiery will; the next, the faculty of permitting his passions to master his reason; and the next, how to hew to the letter to his own ideas of gallantry, courage, and loyalty to his friends. Opposed to Hotspur is a young prince who has avoided the responsibilities to his father and to England because of his concern with wine, women, and song, and because of a unique psychology that expresses itself in carefully maneuvering for a sudden entrance into a world of favor and approval. His is a nature which seldom permits self-deception, which makes his reason master of his passions, and which enables him to realize, at any time, a hierarchy of values. Such realization enables him to keep latent the knowledge of what he must eventually make patent, the acceptance of his royal responsibilities.

Although Shakespeare uses drama as a form to communicate through *realism* the experiences of real people in real life situations, he is, above all, talking of mankind. Each quality in Hotspur, Falstaff, Hal, the King, Glendower, and the others in the play, reflects truths of man's nature. The play, as with every particular literary work, does not deny the nature of mankind, but shows how qualities and intensity differ among the specific individuals. What the experience of each individual reveals to himself and to his fellowman, either in life or in its literary illusion, image, or delusion, is that he differs, and differs mainly because he does not have all of the facets of each quality which constitutes an essence of man. Hotspur is not entirely devoid of rational qualities: at least he knows that the nature of woman is such that his wife, a unique individual among all women, is not likely to keep any communication secret from everyone. While Hal is primarily rational, he is not without a certain number of qualities which make up his volitional nature. His latent royal qualities prevent his being as warm and spontaneous in responses as a commoner might be. With Shakespeare there is always the concept that disaster strikes when man makes passions lord of his reason; when acts are too hasty, too rash, too ill-advised.

So much for essence, generally. We close this part of the discussion by noting that all branches of knowledge, of spiritual beliefs, and physical theory have rested on the nature, the essence, or the definition of mankind.

Essence and Existence

MATERIALISM

Although they agreed on the basic nature of man, there have been different schools of thought as to the relative importance of the different aspects of man. In a literary sense these are romanticism, rationalism, naturalism, and classicism. We shall relate these to the large view from which all literature must spring. Concerning man's nature, he has made several premises: *Natura sive Deus* (Nature is Absolute); Nature is herself God—naturalism. Nature takes the place of a traditional God who is outside man and nature. Physical nature becomes the basis and supreme measure of all experience. This belief is at the heart of Russian communism. The traditional God is reduced to nature and the Creator to the created. In a primitive form, this premise was inherent in the works of Anaximander (611–545 B.C.), Heraclitus (540–480 B.C.), and Parmenides (515–456 B.C.). The doctrine was refined by Democritus (460–370 B.C.). In *De Rerum Natura,* a fine anticipation of the modern atomic theory, Lucretius (98–55 B.C.) developed a strong case for naturalism. The influence of Christianity with its transcendent God and its immanent Christ checked the thesis of naturalism.

The explosion that was the Renaissance (commencing in the fourteenth century) dealt crushing blows to a church which had embraced in its authority the total essence of man—his mental, spiritual, and physical faculties. Ironically, the Renaissance spirit of classicism, in the sense of our earlier discussions, which was characterized by harmonious exercise of reason, will, and materiality, gave rise to a spirit that would destroy that unity of personality. The intrepid personalities of the Renaissance discovered through the arts and through anatomy the human body, an aspect of man the Church had been happy to play down. The spirit of the explorers enlarged the sense of the physical bounds of the universe. Furthermore, research brought to light earlier theories of Greek thinkers: Plato, Aristotle, Anaxagoras, Democritus, Lucretius, and many others. The printing press, instruments of navigation, and gunpower made the world infinitely more horizontal and fastened man's attention on the material world of immediacy. With the impact on the world of things, on the macroscopic nature of the physical universe, the scene was ripe for the first of the modern materialists, François Rabelais. Rabelais was not only a materialist, but he also had a literary power. From Rabelais and his concerns with the immediacy of the physical universe were born such literary and philosophical terms as *pantheism, cosmocentrism, naturalism, empiricism,* and *materialism.* Man began to pass from wonder, which had become infinitely great, to fright at a world whose apparent infinite expansion served but to make man more microscopic in his own eyes. Rabelais' work was carried on in literary and in pedagogical circles by Jean Jacques Rousseau.

This materialism has passed down to this century through the writing and thought of Karl Marx, Leo Tolstoy, Konstantonovna Krupskaya, wife of Lenin, and Anatoli Vassilyrvich Lunacharski (1875–1933), minister of education under Lenin. One of the main difficulties in communicating with the Russians concerning democracy is our lack of understanding of their basic philosophy: Nature is Absolute! Russian writing reflects this philosophy. The writing of Hemingway, Steinbeck, Baldwin, Tennessee Williams, Dreiser, Norris, London, and Dos Passos is saturated with an inherent naturalism. The reader is referred to works by these authors and to a consideration of the excellent book, Leslie Fiedler's *Love and Death in the American Novel*. The difference between the American writers and the continental writers is that the American expresses his naturalism through Freud rather than through philosophy. This first philosophical premise concerning the principal reality—nature as absolute, the world of the material—is countered by the second, that of humanism.

RATIONALISM

In the second great philosophical premise, we have *Homo sive Deus*. Man, a reasonable being, is absolute, is God incarnate. He is the unique master of himself and of the universe. (The only modern American expression of this rational premise in literature is from Ayn Rand in her *The Fountainhead* and *Atlas Shrugged*.) The earliest Western expression of this philosophy includes some of the greatest figures: Plato, Aristotle, and Marcus Aurelius. This humanistic force was absorbed and moderated in the Christian Church, a church which would assume that man could be god-like, but not God. The same force that liberated the force of naturalism also restored the humanistic temperament. Humanism means that man's reason is sufficient to reveal himself to himself, to others, and the universe to himself. During the Renaissance, the German Ulrich von Hutten, the Dutch Erasmus, and the Englishmen John Colet and William Lily set the stage for a force as deadly to the Christian vertical world as was the first premise of "Nature Is Absolute."

From the Renaissance humanists or rationalists have evolved

such terms as *deists, rationalists, occasionalists, ontologists, fideists, immaterialists,* and *pan-idealists.* These terms are current in modern philosophy, psychology, art, and literature. An understanding of the terms makes for greater ease in understanding current expression and current rational trends. Pushing reason to the extreme, the philosophy of man as a measure of all values was taken over by Hegel, by Gentile, and, disastrously, by Mussolini. This philosophy was at the heart of the Fascists' political and social philosophy—and an integral expression of what the Christian Church has dreaded as the greatest sin of all, the sin of pride. This is the unforgivable sin in Hawthorne's *The Scarlet Letter,* in which three great sins —the revealed, the concealed, and the unforgivable—are evaluated so that Chillingworth's is the most horrible. Other terms that are common to the second premise are *humanism, anthropocentrism,* and *essentialism.* In its extreme form, this philosophy will overthrow body and spirit in the name of reason. Such a philosophy has been prevalent in America only during the Puritan Period. Modern educators representing humanism in America are Hutchins, Harry Broudy, Arthur Bestor, and Russell Kirk. Their influence is more in the area of educational philosophy than elsewhere.

Reliance on the intellect, on man's rational faculties, has not been a significant American phenomenon. However, the greatest American and English institutions of learning have been humanistic: Harvard, Yale, Princeton, California at Berkeley, Amherst, Stanford, Williams, Trinity, Smith, Vassar, and Radcliffe—among others in America—and the great English universities of London, Cambridge, and Oxford. Significantly, the institutions mentioned have furnished relatively little current literature.

ROMANTICISM

But the third premise has struck America shrewd blows. In the third premise we have *Societas sive Deus:* Society is the absolute, is God incarnate! (By the use of "God" in this book, we are not referring to God as a religious figure only, but as a word that includes the controlling force of all of man's personality.) Historically, the idea that society—the group, the state—is the measure of all things had its inception in Sparta. Although the rational spirit was powerful in Rome, romanticism was strong enough to reflect the feeling that wherever a Roman stood, Rome existed as a holy manifestation. Shaw was not far off the truth when he equated Joan of Arc in his *St. Joan* as a force of nationalism, a nationalism that was to make France conscious of herself as a sacred manifestation as a nation, apart and independent of the Holy Roman Empire. Nationalism is a matter of will, volition. Artists and writers, because of their unique individualities, have poured out much protest against this premise, which enslaves them in the name of a society which claims for itself the nature of creator. Significant is the fact that few writers have supported the thesis; the majority have rebelled against its strictures.

This theory was first advanced in the field of education, art, and sociology by such writers as John Fichte (1762–1814), Emile Durkheim (1858–1917), Ernst Kriech (1882), and Alfred Baumlet (1887). The rallying cry for Germany in her wars of 1870, 1914 and 1939 was *Der Staat is de präsente Gott* (The State is god incarnate). The philosophy is at the heart of Nazi philosophy, of racism, and collectivism. It manifested itself in the United States as "McCarthyism." In the nineteenth century, the premise appeared as romanticism in art, philosophy, and literature, and as socialism in politics. The government control of public utilities and facilities is a manifestation of this premise; social security, medical care, control of railways, radio, and television are reflections of its partial but creeping influence. A traditional God has been all but eliminated in politics, art, and literature in the name of the state and its institutions, institutions that are universally becoming more paternalistic. The cost of ridding oneself of the God of traditional Christianity and Judaism has been the necessity for the state to become that which has been removed.

What is significant is that this third premise involves will, spirit, the emotive life of man, and his irrational qualities. The creation of the state and the group as the supreme forces necessarily destroys the individual in making him herd-like in manner. He is forced to rely on the animal instincts of seeking his needs in the company of his fellow animals. The nature of mankind is that he may worship together; he may brawl together; he may fight together; but he thinks alone. The crucial part of this discussion emerges when we realize that the price of surrendering himself to the group is to submit to the world of the irrational. From this premise have come the terms *sociocentric, socialistic, activistic,* and *irrational*. In the field of politics and social relationships, the most negative results are those brought about by the philosopher and flag-waver Fichte, by the state-centered Hans Günther, down to the notorious minister of education for Hitler, Alfred Rosenberg (1893–1946). In the United States the influence was most marked in education: the platoon system, the activity theory, and the philosophy of John Dewey, together with its frightening misinterpretations, have done through the schools what politics and war were accomplishing in continental Europe. Philosophers Charles Peirce, George Mead, and William James also supported this premise. Educational supporters of this sociocentrism involve H. Gor-

don Hullfish, Florence B. Stratemeyer—"life adjustment,"
—and Theodore Brameld.

The Modern Dilemma

Some small reflection should indicate that the artist and
writer of today is caught in a dilemma. Being primarily individualistic, he is caught between two deadly and conflicting
essences of man: the materiality inherent in the first premise of
naturalism—nature is absolute—and the third premise which
says that society is itself a God. He has no freedom in either
direction. Because art and literature are not *per se* essentially
rationalistic, he has few weapons with which to fight. He has
retreated in desperation to existentialism. Logically, the first
response of the artist is to protest and to solve the problem.
Giraudoux, Anouilh, Salacrou, Sartre, and Camus have attempted to do so by showing the irrational parts of current
society; they have done so by reason, ironically. Because the
modern audiences have forsaken reason, their efforts have been
but moderately successful.

Another group of influential dramatists—Beckett, Adamov,
Ionesco, Genet, Albee, Pinter, and Simpson—has seen that the
logical approach is fruitless. These members of the Theatre of
the Absurd, instead of protesting what the conflicting premises
have done to man since the Renaissance, are satisfied to reveal
the senselessness of man—cut off, first, from a traditional God,
next from a logical certitude, and finally condemned to the
herd-like subordination to the group, to the state. Since, traditionally, language had been used to synthesize as well as to
express man's mental, volitional, and material entities, these
dramatists realized that the usual language no longer had

meaning. Thus they use traditional terms in such a way as to show that they are so absurd as to have no rational meaning. That is so because the meaning is not in the word, but in the person who uses the word. Because man's personality has been dichotomized—as man he seems a contradiction to the essence of mankind—since he is a contradiction, he and his words are absurd. This movement is yet to strike the American theatre with full force.

A useful approach to the modern problem is to recognize that the writers of the nineteenth century, primarily Browning and Tennyson, saw conflict and offered a solution, however inadequate. The American and English writers of the early part of the century—from Hardy through Galsworthy, Eliot, and Sinclair Lewis—saw the conflict, highlighted the conflict, but gave no solution. The sophisticated members of the Theatre of the Absurd and our own "beatniks" recognize the sense-lessness of *a* man whose intellectual, spiritual, and material qualities are irretrievably sundered, through a rejected God, through a declining reason, and through a malignant nature. To them, man is useless because the integral parts which make him man no longer have any intercommunication.

The conflicts that writers have seen, traditionally, are those brought about by such struggles as church versus state, industrialism versus the desire to avoid its ugly physical manifestations, specializations in mass production versus craftsmanship, authoritarianism versus democracy, the liberal attitude versus the conservative point of view, the impact of evolution on traditional religious institutions, and the assertion of primacy of one aspect of man's personality as related to the others: mind, spirit, and body. Despite the intensity of such conflicts which have raged not only between two forces but within each, such as intrareligious squabbles, the controversies have been over matters of degrees as to how much one force can exercise control over others.

Tennyson did not deny the claims and urgency of science. He saw the conflict that must result when man's intimate and personal relationships with God were threatened by the feeling that man loses his uniqueness when he is not directly established as God's prize creation, but is the tag end of a biological development from lower forms. T. S. Eliot's *The Wasteland* does not deny the worlds of mind, spirit, and body, but does decry the fact that modern man is not willing to face the challenge of establishing new relationships among the essences of man. He did not deny that the values that man had traditionally accepted could be in error. He was infuriated because man was destroying his sensibility; by *sensibility* we mean an intense spiritual feeling about the validity of living an individual life through examining the highest life as interpreted through traditional religious and educational beliefs. Man no longer is able to articulate his language as sense and sensibility.

We learn by seeing and hearing differences among different experiences and among the effects different experiences have on people. Because the main emphases of existentialism are psychological and literary, we shall approach our task more closely—and fruitfully—by discriminating among naturalistic, romantic, and existential qualities on the literary scene.

Before we do so, however, we need to consider the human faculty for categorizing experience over time. Whether the existentialist considers being "human" such a common denominator, or not, is one matter. However, his writings admit the fact that he has the faculty for considering and expressing experience as myth, legend, and symbol.

Myth, Legend, and Symbol

In returning to the question of language as significant, we stress that words have the meanings that give their essences. That is, in the same way that man has a nature which distinguishes him from other objects of experience, each word will have a nature which will distinguish itself from another word: *ink* has a denotation that by its very qualities cannot be *milk*. Having defined the word in the light of the qualities that make the word unique, the word is then a sign in the universal sense. We need no specific arguments between any two individuals on separate occasions to agree that ink is ink and milk is milk. True, there may be individual differences concerning the use to which these words are put. The other important aspect of language is that of symbol. Much of the language is symbolic in that the meaning that is given a word or term must result from specific agreements among human individuals as to what is represented. In speaking of ink as a mixture and as one of unique properties, unique enough to make ink a complete value in itself, *ink* becomes a sign. However, in order to give the innumerable combinations of man's mind, heart, and hand the most complete expression, specific agreements are made that a word can have more than one meaning. *Ink* can stand not only for the physical sign of an object, but can represent the entire human act. "With a few drops of ink the history of the world was changed." In this instance *ink* is extended so that the physical nature is expanded to rational and emotional areas. Over time, man at a particular time and on specific occasions enters into formal and informal agreements that a word can be given more than one level of meaning. The same process occurs with the symbol. A cross—as sign—represents two objects fastened together at an angle. *Cross,* by agreements of certain individuals or societies of individuals, also can mean trials and tribulations. *Cross* can also be made to mean the total personality of Christ.

Traditionally, in literature, myth, fable, and legend, symbols have been carried down to give continuity to the meaning of physical, intellectual, and spiritual experiences of individuals and individual societies. Writers have relied on the belief that a symbol used over and over again would even become a sign— as *east* is *birth*—and that successive societies would continue to accept, within limits, agreed-upon meanings as symbols. From the inception of our Western literature with Homer, signs and symbols have been in the light of what was believed to be the true nature of mankind. The modification of the symbols over years has reflected, until now, only a shift in the emphasis given among the parts that constitute man's nature. In Gilbert Highet's work *The Classical Tradition,* the author observes:

> Our modern world is in many ways a continuation of the world of Greece and Rome. Not in all ways—particularly not in medicine, music, industry, and applied science. But in most of our intellectual and spiritual activities we are the grandsons of the Romans, and the great-grandsons of the Greeks.

That we are so results from the fact that we have been willing to accept myth, legend, fable, sign, and symbol as expressing, as the Greeks and Romans did, the essence of man. Whether a myth is historical, philosophical, or the result of the observations of the working of physical phenomena in physical nature, myth and legend represent people who, essentially, have the qualities that make them human. When T. S. Eliot refers to myths, Grail legends, and classical figures such as Tiresias, he does so deliberately, to communicate a sense of unbroken historical communication of the truths of mankind.

In his excellent chapter "The Reinterpretation of Myths," Highet opens his discussion by pointing out that Sigmund Freud realized that man's view of mankind and of himself also comes from enduring, everlasting expressions of myth and legend. Freud claimed that these expressions are manifested as powerful instincts concerning the elemental essences of man such as jealousy, love, self-adoration, and hatred. From the acceptance of the language of myth and legend have been derived such terms as "Oedipus Complex," the "Electra Complex," and "Narcissism." Jung pointed out that myths *must* perpetuate themselves because they represent not so much one man as they do the deepest beliefs and emotions about the human race.

Through all recorded myths, legends, and historical accounts of man there run the two main streams of evidence of man as created by a divine and superior force, and of man as creating his own god. The more he senses within himself his being made by a powerful and transcendent external force, the more he feels that force within himself. He believes that he has much of the divinity in his own person. At the same time, the more he senses what he has within himself as divine, the more he is tempted to define his creator in his—man's—own terms. First, man asserts his superiority over the lower animals. Then he asserts his superior powers over members of his own society, believing, all the time, that he is of superior material. He has more of the divine within himself than they have. At this point, he becomes *tragic*.

Admitting that all of his fellow men come from the same creator, he finds in himself more divine stuff than they have. In asserting his individualism over his society, he claims a divinity greater than, collectively, other members of his society, are willing to admit. Eventually he is destroyed. In the greater heights of tragedy, the tragic hero asserts his own sense of power against the power that created him—a god, or the gods. Here, he strikes at the very essence of the supernatural power. He walks on the purple carpets of the gods, and, like Agamemnon, he is destroyed.

When man is an *epic,* or *epical,* he does not revolt against his society, or against the gods—at least against those on his side. He carries out the wishes of his own society. He possesses the qualities most admired by the people of his time. Thus, he is encouraged to continue his life, *as long* as he represents what his own people admire, and what they desire to have perpetuated. So, an epic tends to be long, a tragedy short. Neither society nor the gods will permit a long revolt.

Now, the epic hero does fall, eventually. He does so not through opposing his society, but because he carries out its wishes. The epic hero dies because he prefers to lead his society in its own desires, which could, at times, be other than his own. One significant difference in the myth of the epic and that of the tragedy is that in the epic, society demands and welcomes another epic hero, much like the first. In tragedy, society desires no more tragic heroes.

The epic hero represents the physical, intellectual, and emotive proportions demanded by any one society at any one time. However, society's values change over time. The epic hero of yesterday would be the tragic hero of today, if he asserted his basic qualities. The aggressive, heroic, and bold epic figure of World War II would be rejected today. In an age that rejects his qualities, today's epic hero—except for Sunday afternoon football—is, compared to yesterday's, an "anti-epic." This phenomenon can be seen in such productions as *The Fugitive.*

Now we return to our previous statement that today the will, mind, and matter have passed the point of asserting primacy among each other. That which makes up man has resulted in the denial by each of the other two: by reason, of body and will; by will, of body and mind; and by the material, of the intellectual and the spiritual. Man has become absurd in his own eyes. He looks with horror and emits bitter laughter at the dissociated intellect, will, and body. Whatever meaning he can find must be found in each man for its own sake. In pointing out that life is absurd, the writers have had to use available signs and symbols. Because man has turned aside from essentialism, from his willingness to accept man as defined in the light of mind, will, and senses acting together, with no experience complete except in the light of the three, he must revise his use of myth.

Seeing man destroyed by a Hitlerian will that completely denied the material and intellectual world, and by a Russian materialism that denied the world of spirit and intellect, and by a weakening rational spirit not capable of interpreting a world of physical change to mankind, Albert Camus wrote *The Myth of Sisyphus*. Instead of using Sisyphus to show the intrepid spirit of the Sisyphus who tried to defy the gods, Camus shows the rebel as one who sees the fruitlessness in striving to do what cannot be done. Camus decided that we cannot be tragic or epic today because we are so concerned with one particular part of man that we do not see that our tasks are hopeless. Because we no longer know what is tragic or epical, we are absurd. That is, we are no longer human. Camus, as with members of the Theatre of the Absurd, has a solution. Man must realize his lack of tragic or heroic stature, but through struggling, even though only to an inevitable defeat, he will eventually conquer. The triumph comes in the recognition and the struggle. Apparently, man is absurd because he can never win; he is absurd because he no longer desires to be tragic or epical; he is absurd because he has forgotten that although man can never be a god, he can never realize what mankind is unless he approaches being god—insofar as his body, heart, and hand permit.

Removing man's powerful belief and faith in traditional religions and certitudes has freed him from many problems, particularly from that of devoting his life to a course based on the nature of a god not physically demonstrable. Man is able to cut all that does not relate to the physical world of things and people, together with ideas and feelings about the world of things and people. He is paying a terrible price in at least one respect. He was frustrated by never being able to deal personally with god or gods, but he was conscious of a divine power that grew, inevitably, by his need to be god-like, to aspire to the qualities and demands inherent in his supernatural qualities. Today, man must look out at the world of other men. By definition, they are like him. In a horizontal world, moral, intellectual, and physical superiority are not as evident among men as they are between man and his gods. In cutting off a god, a god in the traditional sense, man has cut off his past and his future. He has reduced himself to the intellectual, emotional, and sensory immediate world of fellow men. He has more time to concern himself with his fellow man, but his concern has not given him satisfaction. Whereas he has had a traditional world of myth, legend, religion, political theory, and ethical guides, today he has eliminated his supernatural concepts. What standard can *A* now use to evaluate his fellow man *B?* Where can a yardstick be derived? What has resulted is that man has de-evaluated himself as the measure of the values of experience by handing this role over to naturalism, which considers man as only one manifestation of the only reality, the physical universe. If he does not take the escape through naturalism, he is forced to existentialism in which each specific person is the sole judge of the total world of experience and is so entirely in terms of the self—*existentialism*.

Question of Certitude

INFALLIBILITY REJECTED

Traditionally, man has used his fellow man through specified relationships to reach God; in William Blake's poetry, man uses God to reach man; in modern literature man is represented as having abandoned God as goal or means to another goal. In this abandonment modern man has succeeded in dehumanizing himself in admitting the entire superiority of naturalism: in reaching the position of naturalism, our modern man has had to give up the concept of God as an end or as a process. In such a surrender, man has also sacrificed his humanity. Our comment on naturalism has discussed this phenomenon. If he has not embraced naturalism, man tries to save himself by being creator and created, in existentialism. He states his own essence in his own terms, holding experience outside himself to yield but tentative truths and holding his own response to experience as temporary and tentative.

In Stephen Pepper's most influential book, *World Hypotheses,* all dogmatism is rejected—that of spirit, that of intellect, and even that in naturalism. Pepper opens his theses by stating:

> Belief is a naïve attitude, while doubt is an acquisition won through long and hard experience. . . .
> A dogmatist is one whose belief exceeds his cognitive grounds for belief.

The three premises we have noted—nature as absolute, reason as absolute, and society as absolute—Pepper would sweep away as dogma. He concludes, correctly, that the positions are held with more belief than is rationally justified. We can see that he is setting up one of two positions: either he is advocating a return to the synthesis of will, reason, and senses; or he is preparing the way for the individual to hold beliefs that can be permanent only insofar as the evidence for the belief equals the strength of the belief to the individual. While man may have allowed will, reason, and senses to fall apart in the light of any coherent philosophy of life, he finds that he cannot abolish their reality. The fact that he denies at least two in his insistence of the primacy of the third does not mean that man can arbitrarily destroy the essence he denies. Pepper, stressing, as is obvious, a return to reason as guide, stumbles over the matter of conviction. Attitude involves the emotional part of man, his will. Pepper agrees that the attitude of a belief is stronger than the evidence on which the belief is founded! Thus, a mediocre student who is convinced that he will become better has better grounds to believe that he will improve than one who is not so convinced. What is involved here is the great truth that conviction—through will—will provide the very evidence that gives good ground for belief. In short, we are justified in concluding that the will to believe is itself a rational basis for belief.

The refusal of the modern educator to generalize, the refusal of the modern writer to leave his world of "realistic details," and the insistence on never leaving the world of concrete objects reflect the modern disease of ultradogmatism—dogmatism as indicated through the three premises detailed in this chapter. Traditionally, the essence of mankind is the one great generalization. Ultadogmatism is characterized, as Pepper indicates correctly, by the fact that a dogmatist will not generalize; he will not work in the light of general principles. Why not? If he generalized, he would not be a dogmatist! Pepper's language on this point is that among accepted criteria of belief there is one which if generalized would lead the dogmatist to the acceptance of beliefs or degrees of belief which he now refuses to accept. So, explicitly he acknowledges cognitive criteria which he implicitly denies. Historically, dogmatism has arisen through a movement away from emphasis on the total personality of man to emphasis on individual interpretations of man's personality. These interpretations have come about so as to enforce the theory held as "infallible."

If some view of man can be considered "infallible," the appeal to authority satisfies that part of men that seeks security. We note this truth when our advertising uses those individuals who are so famous as to gain the position of making expert declarations. We are happy to appeal to their infallibility in confirming our emotions, sensory experiences, and beliefs. We shall see that the dilemma of the existentialist is grim. At least in naturalism there is the infallibilty of the elemental bits of matter as god; in existentialism, the individual can appeal only to his own authority for confirmation. The doctrine of infallibility of ecclesiastical pronouncements has been under powerful attack for centuries. The irony is that can we state, with sufficient reasonable evidence, that the appeal to the self as infallible is no more valid than the infallibility of church doctrines. In short, are we not using infallibility when we assert that infallibility is totally wrong? Small wonder that Salinger's Holden Caulfield found no certainty in the world other than his own, that he found his world of experience to be "phony."

Leaving the area of "infallibility," which is primarily in the matters of the will, the emotions, and the volitional part of man, consider the question of *certainty*. Certainty began to replace infallibility with the onset of the Renaissance. Certainty has been composed of two main factors: evidence of the fact—the thing itself—and principles verifiable through human reason—such as mathematical principles.

With the world made more horizontal by the impacts of reason and science from the fourteenth century on, man concluded that while religious infallibility—the vertical infallibility—might be in for rough sledding, the certainty of natural laws and mathematical truths was sufficient authority. In modern times mathematicians are said to have admitted that no longer can they hold out a claim for certainty in the field of mathematical speculation. A truer statement would be that they have not so much discovered that the principles they have used before to be wrong as much as they have discovered other principles more generalized in scope and validity. Even Pepper seems to have overlooked the fact that mathematics as idea is an irrefutable certainty in the sense of being a total law for measuring the world in a quantitative sense. By the same token, religious experience is a certainty. Quite likely, the principles urged as infallible and uncertain are not so much in error as they are incomplete in view of higher principles not discovered as operative.

CERTITUDE CHALLENGED

The purpose of this discussion is to indicate that the same uncertainty that has been urged against the certitude of science and reason and the same fallibility that has been asserted against the views of infallibility are now a part of foreign policy, economic theory, social relationships, and educational theory. At the heart of existentialism, as we shall see in some detail, the individual is isolated from external certainty and infallibilty. Why then, since infallibilty and certainty are out of style, do we believe as certainty "experts" and "experts'" advertising?

One significant reason is that modern man is so torn with doubt through conflicting appeals to will, mind, and body that he will accept what an expert claims to be true, not because what is said is true, but because man believes that the expert will speak only what he, the expert, believes to be truth. Another reason is that modern man seeks security: what the expert asserts that agrees with the frame of reference of our modern man will confirm his importance to himself; whatever does not fit his frame of reference will be rejected because the expert now becomes one who is not an authority, but a transmitter of information which he, the expert, has obtained elsewhere. Even he, the expert, "can make an error"— "Everyone makes mistakes."

Now, the artists and literary people are concerned because they know that what they *feel* to be certain is generally so. Because of their artistic natures they not only desire to know— a quality of mankind—but they also have an intense desire to know. They are moved with the high degree of intensity we mentioned earlier. Like Descartes, our artists never leave the position that a man and mankind are complicated; their experiences are also complicated. They insist that some judgment be made about all men and certain men. A significant difference between a poet and a philosopher is that the poet will never rest until through heart, hand, and mind he gives meaning to mankind through particularizations in the light of specific people and their specific experiences. The philosopher will bring the truth to man and leave the truth as principles, not moved into action through any named individuals in the light of thoughts, feelings, and senses. Another difference is that while the philosopher speaks through his mind about mind, will, and body, the poet expresses through heart, hand, and body the nature of man.

MODERN VIEWS

The artist who renders the general concrete must speak to the condition of man today. He can diagnose; he can prescribe; he may despair, but he must, by his nature, view man and his inner and outer experiences. If the writer gives up the vertical world for the horizontal world, he will look more to relationships interman and intraman. He may become, like Brecht, an exponent of the Epic Theatre and will view man as isolated from God, but as meaningful only in social and political relationships with his fellow man. He may be an existentialist like Sartre or Camus: in such a case man must stand outside and must be alienated from supernatural and human relationships. He may be like Faulkner and reveal man as decadent, fractured, and disinherited through the collapse of traditional eschatology and through the decay of his cultural institutions. Or he may be like Robert Lowell and view man as obliged to create within himself the world of mind, spirit, and body. Since a curtain has fallen between external infallibilty in a religious sense and individual man who must, because he is a man, share from the general store represented by mankind, Lowell tries to solve the problem by having each person intuitively aware of what constitutes a man. This intuition, working in confused and hazy fashion, is strong enough to keep man's personality intact. Man knows that he has wandered from the great truths, but he has a sufficient awareness and intensity of and to them that he can find his way back to the supernatural.

Whether he is an essentialist like T. S. Eliot, Graham Greene, Flannery O'Connor, John Cheever, and Ayn Rand, or whether he is an existentialist like Salinger, Sartre, and Camus, the modern writer is caught, by his role as writer, in an unenviable position. Having a greater sensitivity to personality than most people and having the need for his "super-colossal" ego to be nourished and nurtured—even when we live in a time when the ego receives no small adulation—the existentialist writer agonizes because of his isolation from mankind and because he knows that naturalism has more than imaginary potentialities to still him forever. The essentialist is not in a much better position because he has to equate the essence of man as sufficiently great to contend with, and to make life worth contending with, the impersonal and unhearing voice of scientific phenomena.

A final observation completes our present line of thought. Because man has abandoned the supernatural, and thus has tossed away the major part of his tragic nature, his stature has decreased. Arthur Miller, valiantly but pitifully, tries to present prose and drama in support of a thesis that man can be a tragic figure when viewed in the context of relationships with his fellow man. "Pain and suffering are enough," cries Miller. We do not believe him; he has failed to sell his product. He has failed for more than one reason. Man's esteem of man is now so low that the idea of revolt is ridiculous. Part of the stature of traditional tragedy was that man revolted against a force which he hated, but which he respected—and one which he acknowledged as superior because of its supernatural nature. Miller is wrong in claiming that a person can have stature today. Man surrendered that, not on grounds of rank or position, when he tossed away his spiritual dimension.

The satirical note of the modern French dramatist is the better approach. Comedy is of this world, of a world of illusion and delusion. Since pretense, misunderstanding, and the microcosmic are fields for satire, perhaps that is the correct medium for modern writing.

We know that man has placed himself in the temporal world where he must come to terms with naturalism, must return to the traditional view of man, or must enter the world of self, of existentialism. Returning to a review of our three premises, the first shows that mind and spirit are rejected on behalf of nature and the world of the senses; the second would reject the senses and spirit for reason and the mind; the third opposes the world of matter, the world of mind, and does so for the sake of society and action. Restating our points for greater clarity, consider the psychological position of each of the three philosophies:

1. *Percipio, ergo sum* (Bacon, Helvetius, Marx, Lenin, Lunacharski). I perceive; therefore, I am. This point is the starting point of naturalism, empiricism, and materialism.
2. *Cogito, ergo sum* (Descartes, Berkeley, Payne, Hegel, Gentile). I think; therefore, I am. This facet is the starting point of anthropocentrism, rationalism, and idealism.
3. *Ago, ergo sum* (Fichte, John Dewey, Kerchensteiner). I act; therefore, I am. This position is the starting point of sociocentrism, activism, and pragmatism.

Essence and essentialism are embraced by:

Percipio, ergo sum;
Cogito, ergo sum;
Ago, ergo sum.

The essence of man is that he perceives; he thinks; he acts; and, therefore, he exists. He is an individual because he perceives, thinks, and acts—because he has the essence of man.

The Fourth Premise: Existentialism

The fourth premise, existentialism, denies the nature of man as being an individual man who exists because of seeing, thinking, and acting. The existentialist reverses the order by stating:

Sum (vivo, existo), ergo percipio, cogito, ago.
I am (I live, I exist) therefore I perceive, I think, and I act.

First you live and exist; then you think! The existentialists say, then, *"Primo vivere postea philosophare"*: "Existences precede essence." This school is in revolt against the three initial premises, as we have noted earlier. Leaders in the existential movement number Sören Kierkegaard, Gogarten, Thurneyson, Karl Barth, Emil Brunner, Grisbach, Lavelle, Lesenne, Sartre, Simone de Beauvoir, Camus, Wahl, Berdyayev, Kafka, Marcel and Wust. In educational circles the existential movement is known as the Life Adjustment Principle. The reader should read Florence Stratemeyer's *Education for Life Adjustment*. In the name of pure existing, performing the primitive cell functions, the individual abolishes will, sense, and senses in the thesis *Nihil sive Deus*—Nothingness is absolute and the measure of all things! Psychologically, we have represented the nature of the premise that the immediate concerns of everyday living for the individual are more important than reference to traditional values of man's total personality of mind, heart, and body. In specific terms, this life principle consists of keeping well, understanding self, and adjusting to the natural environment. "What shall I eat?" "What is the best diet for me?" "How shall I select someone to aid me in realizing my needs and goals?"

The move from infallibility to certitude—a movement whose inception was in the fifteenth- and sixteenth-century work of Francis Bacon, Copernicus, and later in the work of Newton—and the turning aside from certitude in the twentieth century were aided by the philosophical and scientific thoughts that stated that the evolution of the world was through blind chance. All life is merely the struggle of blind chance and blind forces. There is no order of the world in the sense of man's traditional view of the nature of man. As we have noted, man is sufficiently shocked by the powerful claims of an impersonal order of science that reduces the world of living and nonliving objects to a hundred or so kinds of atoms, that he concerns himself only with the existence of individual people.

THE EXISTENTIAL MAN

The seeds of existentialism were sown earlier than the twentieth century, however. They needed only the proper environment for sprouting. What is the proper environment for a trend which places all of its efforts and emphases on "existence," rather than on "essence"?

Briefly, existentialism comes to the fore when knowledge is not valued according to any external truth or to any standard regarded as verifiable. Instead, the only knowledge is that which the individual is conscious of as subject, not object, and which consciousness is freed of emotions, of social truths as objective truths, of mathematical laws as obligatory, and of religious strictures as binding. What makes up knowledge and its source as knowledge is a matter of consciousness for each single person in a unique and personal sense. There are no different external and internal worlds for the individual. These worlds are not different because all that can be examined apart from the mind can be examined within the mind.

The existentialist shakes off any idea that man can be rational. Like Freud, he believes that man relies on the desire to live with his delusions. He would rather be superstitious than truthful. Thus, state the existentialists, "man is absurd." To show him as absurd is to pave the way for existentialism. However, the existentialist is hurt both ways because he is also absurd as an existentialist. To be free, he must make a choice that consciously condemns himself to pain, agony, and isolation. He is thrown back to the position of the essentialist who cried, in his metaphysical poetry, "Be my joy three parts pain." Man suffers, traditionally, much of his delusion in being forced to make distinctions between the physical and psychological worlds, but the refusal to distinguish between these two worlds is a fatal weakness in existentialism as a philosophy: its position is simply untenable, philosophically. Thus, Genet's world of phantasy is a true picture of the ultraexistentialist.

While we have traced the decline of essentialism from its high-water mark of the Renaissance to the current low ebb of this our present era, we must realize—always—that quietly, subtly, insidiously, but effectively, philosophy itself directs these trends. Kant tried to synthesize systematically a philosophy which would take into account the new truths of the *Enlightenment*. He made what is viewed as nigh well a fatal error. He stated that the mind must depend upon certain principles which can not be obtained from sense experience. Since they can not come from sensory experience, they must have existed prior to each man, as *a priori*. He called such truths *transcendental*. These truths are free, cause-wise, from all sensory materials. He was doing "rather well" until he came to "God," "immortality," and a "total universe."

Without involving ourselves too deeply in Kant's tortuous, if brilliant, reasoning, we must observe that he saved faith at the cost of knowledge. He sacrificed the world of knowledge for the world of faith. Giving up knowledge is giving up a major part of essentialism. The defect in Kant's philosophy became more patent with the rise of Marxism and the increase of materialism in all its forms. In 1886 Nietzsche struck swiftly and devastatingly at *a priori* and transcendental assertions. He stated that ideas real to the individual are more important than absolutes, that the power of the will is better than freedom of will, that creativity is an individual matter. To live creatively and with meaning, each strong man must reverse normal values. What is most important is the individual's passing his own judgments, making his own choices, and having courage enough to go beyond traditional moral absolutes, and doing so in the light of instinct, of will.

Since normal values were being reversed by the new scientific and economic orders, Nietzsche's call to the will found ready listeners and responses. Kierkegaard, earlier, had been fighting for religion in another way. Posing a religious irrationalism, he denounced those who believed that reason and man were capable of comprehending God. Because man is an egotist and because he created time to enthrone his egotism, he must always despair because eternity opposes time. Jaspers, Heidegger, Husserl, and Marcel, as philosophers, have had their turns in making the existential mind a philosophy; we shall see with what success.

Incessant conflicts in all human physical, intellectual, and spiritual areas of interest have brought to man's consciousness —and unconsciousness—the feeling and belief that no solution is possible to any specific problem. Social science, physical science, biological science, and economics reveal, but cannot solve. They shy away entirely from such words as *ought, must,* and *should*. Man's traditionals appear to fail man, and he really fails them.

Now, modern man does have an out. But no one wishes to buy or rent any part of the avenue of escape. Man can accept determinism and make as courageous a life as possible. He can assume, with naturalism, that he cannot win, but that he can postpone losing. He can settle for the horizontal level, freeing himself from guilt, suffering, and agony about the next world and his soul. But he would gain additional pressures through the very rejection of a supernatural whose imagined nature and presence offered future alleviation for present agony. He would have to stand or fall on his own visible means of support or nonsupport. He can sacrifice his individuality in favor of a group concept of society. But there is a problem here. Freudianism, itself reflecting some naturalism, poses a grim obstacle. The very personality of man, in the light of *id, ego,* and *super-ego* seems to be so organized, *ab initio* and essentially, that as irrational as man is—and seems to love to be—he seeks to maintain a whole personality. His entire self, distinguishing the subjective world of the mind from the objective world of physical reality, insists that man is conscious of the difference between each.

The desire to maintain an inherent and persistent feeling of individuality forces man to the position of existentialism. He has no other recourse if he is to avoid naturalism. Being honest enough to find no solution to the problems of any form of a life lived as essentialism, he must give up his individuality if he will not adopt naturalism. That form of essentialism can be held only at the price of giving up intellect and spirit, or taking refuge in a group form of social life. Thus, the individual becomes an existentialist. He pays the price for keeping his individuality. He does so at the annihilation of all externals. He throws himself upon himself. What does he believe in?

THE BELIEFS OF THE EXISTENTIAL MAN

1. He opposes romanticism, rationalism, naturalism, classicism.

2. He starts with his own personal philosophy—himself.

3. His deepest feelings are the history of his own personal feelings.

4. He will go to any lengths to develop a history to awaken his consciousness.

5. He is filled with horror and foreboding concerning the predicament of man.

6. The existentialist cares nothing for abstract man: he denies the Greek thinker; he scorns Dewey's social child; he cares only for specific flesh and blood.

7. He cares only for the specific suffering person—himself, a person never free from passion and suffering.

8. He starts with his *Being* because the only Being is his own.

9. He reasons as follows:
   a. To exist is to be caught.
   b. Each person is caught in his own predicament.
   c. Man is always free; he cannot not be free.
   d. He is free because he is the only source of his own acts.
   e. Because each man knows that he must be free and that he is the source of his own acts, he is in anguish, pain, and dread.
   f. Most people try to deny their own freedom. They make believe that they are not free; therefore, they bind themselves with moral bonds which they claim as higher than their wills.
      i. But each man is alone with his own freedom.
      ii. No other man can take this burden, this freedom, from him.
      iii. Not to bind himself to these truths is to be dishonest.

      iv. The alternative to despair with the burden is to act, knowing existence for its own grim nature.

      v. He must never delude himself with hope of eventual success.

      vi. The meaning of his life is to be derived from a continual engagement in a series of choices and acts.

10. Whence comes agony, despair, and anguish?
    a. Reality has its meaning only with the mind of man, but not all reality is in the mind.
    b. The outer world exists as real, but this reality is determined by the consciousness of man in the same way as the inner world is determined.
    c. The existentialist sometimes directs himself toward physical objects, keeping in mind that other people are physical objects.

11. The existentialist desires to achieve a wholeness which is in the reality not in his mind, and he wishes to identify his self with all reality. Yet, he refuses to give up the crucial point of his own self-consciousness. He must yield to that to be made whole.

12. Thus, he is involved in a contradiction. To yield, he must return to the tradition that makes any man partake of the essence of man and to bind himself to such an essence. To surrender his self-consciousness and all mental reality is to turn to naturalism. Thus, all human existence is characterized by a lack of fulfillment, emptiness, and frustration.

13. At least we are, as individuals, free. Coming from the bitterness of an anguish that will always be ours because we can never be whole, is liberty. Each man knows that he must continually choose his own consciousness above complete identity with reality. He is free to despair. No one can nor must take that from him.

14. The existentialist believes that belief is the "consciousness" of believing. Thus there is no belief apart from the choosing and acting of the individual.

15. Sartre's statement is significant: "Choice is possible, but what is not possible is not to choose. I can always choose, but I ought to know that if I do not choose, I am still choosing."

16. There are Christian and atheistic existentialists; however, they have a point in common in that existence comes before essence and that subjectivity is always the point at which any man starts.

17. The atheistic existentialist is not much concerned with whether or not there is a God. The atheistic existentialist would hold that God's existence is not an issue. Each man is only what he does with himself. He has no other law than his own. He exists only as he fulfills himself through the agony of making choices which uphold his own self-consciousness. When man loses this self-consciousness, there is no longer Being, but Nothingness.

18. The conviction of making choices is never one of reason, but one of passion: human existence is passion.

19. The existentialist must make every man aware of his own nature. He must perceive the terrible weight of responsibility on himself.

Thus, we have travelled the introductory road from the Renaissance man to the existentialist of modern everyday life, of the novel, of the screen, and of theatre. Existentialism is here; how long to stay we can not tell. Our starting point was the Renaissance person who, exerting the full weight of mind, body, and spirit, and doing so with the rugged self-sufficient individualism of the total personality, used that total being to demonstrate the essence of man, nature, and God, an essence of which he, an individual, necessarily partook.

Our closing point is the existential man. Denying any debt to the essence of man, even denying man as essential, he chooses himself, the individual man, to demonstrate the only reality—the single choosing self-consciousness. Forcing all reality into himself, he maintains his individuality and solves all problems at the cost of giving himself all reality, divine or otherwise, to bear.

EXISTENTIALISM GENERALLY

We now get down to what makes existentialism tick. In existentialism we find the nature or essence of a thing from its existence; traditionally, we work the other way—existence from essence. Kant pointed out that the nature, the essence, of a sum of money has no bearing on the question of whether or not the sum exists. The understanding of the essence of football has no bearing on whether or not there is a single football team in operation. Yet, if I, a single person, love football, the existence of a football team is important to me. What we can define in a thing is its essence. Existence cannot be defined. Why not? Man has the primacy of heart, hand, and mind; therefore, what can existence be defined from? The reader will do well to try hard to follow this reasoning, for "existence" is difficult to pinpoint.

Essence, the nature of man, has a wealth of structures and relationships. The essence of man involves a participation in will, reason, and senses and does so in varying degrees. A man can be more or less reasonable; thus, he can be more or less of a man. Existence is not analyzable into parts. A thing exists or does not exist; there is no intermediate position between being and not being. The existentialist has a difficult problem; he cannot measure himself nor anyone else from the viewpoint of good, better, best, or little, more, and most.

The movement formally called "Existentialism" came into being during World War I; however, the movement was really a revival of the thought of the Danish writer, Sören Kierke-gaard (1813–1855). This modern existentialism, adapted from Kierkegaard's revolt against the philosophy of Hegel, is not philosophy at all. Instead, the modern existentialism is semi-poetical, semipsychological, and heavily charged with theological implication and controversy. The three varieties of current existentialism are atheistic existentialism, Protestant Biblicism, and Catholic theism. The atheistic type is the only pure type, the only logical type. A denial of the essence of man in terms of mind, will, and spirit can, logically, do no other than to elimi-nate God. Protestant and Catholic existentialism, hopelessly contradictory in theorems, is reflected in the work of Paul Tillich and Jacques Maritain respectively. Nevertheless, despite the distressing confusion of terms among the three forms, there are two unique points of agreement: those of basic conviction and attitude.

A thoroughgoing existentialist claims, with intensity, that the physical concrete world of his own experience is superior to any abstraction (idea), and that no true picture of the world of living can be constructed by man's reason. Thus, the existen-tialist anchors his position on the ground that no general idea is real; no picture of the world of living is real when made by man's reason. Existence is encountered, not thought. In the in-sistence on portraying all experience encountered merely through living, we have had a rash of moving pictures and stage productions on adultery, lesbianism, homosexuality, drug addiction, murder, and every possible exhibition of man's de-pravity. Existentialism is really carrying on the tradition of vi-talism (life adjustment) as represented by Friedrich Nietzsche (1844–1900), Henry Bergson (1859–1941), and Wilhelm Dil-they (1833–1912).

Questioning the existentialist and examining his positions

indicate that there are two main views of existentialism: self-examination and social consideration.

SELF-EXAMINATION AND SOCIAL CONSIDERATION

In each case we are assured that existentialism means an "encounter." By merely living, man encounters life and does so through a conflict of self-examination and also one of social consideration. In the first variety, living is *crisis;* in the second variety, living is encounter which results in *communion.* In American education the second type has been prevailing for some few years; in American literature, existentialism takes the form of crisis, of self-examination. The crisis is also apparent in the current visual arts, television, and movies. In developing the outlines of the types we are discussing, consider the question of money as essence and existence.

The sum of five thousand dollars can be defined in terms of its nature, and can be so done without any proof that such an amount exists. How does the essentialist handle the problem? He looks at his bank account or counts his cash. To prove whether the essence of a term really exists, we use our senses: sight, touch, smell, and hearing. For the traditionalist, existence is shown, in nearly all experience, by the impact of things in a bodily manner, an impact that brings our sensory nature into play. The most logical way to prove and to experience existence would appear to be through the senses; denying the intellect as self-sufficient, the existentialist would seem certain to rely on the senses. He does not, because he is also in retreat before naturalism. One of his main protests is against the theses of naturalism that destroy his view of himself as unique. Self-examination involves a crisis differing from communion (with other people). The insight gathered from the anguish of crisis divorces the existentialist of this type from everyday knowledge. Communion with other people is more rational than the type that exists through crisis. Thus, the existentialism of crisis, of anguished self-examination, is more antirational and more antitraditional than social existentialism. While we can say very little about an existence outside the nature of man, we can say much about the way we go about understanding this existence. Attention must be directed on the human self as the locus of existence where existence is discovered and where existence originates.

The current typical television drama is an excellent example of the anguished self-examination, this critical existentialism that seeks to discover one's existence through an analysis of the self. These dramas are "diluted" by introducing another person who introduces the element of self-discovery through communion with other people. But the main factors are those of encounter, crisis, anguish, and discovery of self as living.

Chapter 3

■

The Philosophy of Existentialism

Introductory

A decision must be made, always, in terms of separating figures and events as to specific areas of knowledge and action. We have little problem in distinguishing psychologists, economists, and geologists. However, we have more of a problem in separating philosophers, psychologists, ethical thinkers, and theologians. Much of their expression is "lyrical" in the sense of combining thinking with feeling. Therefore, we do not separate the less rigorous thinkers such as Sartre and Kierkegaard from the philosophers. While their art is more strongly replete with the literary statement than is true of the others, the other philosophers in the existential tradition are literary in tone. Furthermore, the greatest impetus to thought and the greatest impetus to the entire movement are given by such lyrical figures as Dostoevsky, Sartre, Kierkegaard, and Genet. Thus, we cannot distinguish, in fact, the pure philosophers from the pure artists, other than by degree.

Furthermore, we cannot say that the philosopher came first

in this existential matter. Therefore, we cannot make the chronological division. We cannot arrange them in direct order of their significance because each is significant in a different way. The divisions will be made in terms of religious, social, and literary impacts (admitting the pure arbitrariness of such a classification). In each case, there are strong psychological overtones and undertones in each figure.

The Religious and Ethical Proponents

KARL BARTH

Karl Barth's view of existentialism is oriented toward Protestant-theological thought. He sees that the crisis of anguish and despair can result in the loss of thought so that he achieves a triumph of faith. He finds himself through faith. Through despair, he comes to faith and to a faith in the God of the Old Testament. Here Barth is trying to save God, and he is quite profound. If the sin of pride is the great Christian vice, and if the sin of pride is reliance on one's reason, the destruction of reason will necessarily permit man to avoid this sin and to come close to God and the self. In an important sense, Faulkner's *Light in August* is in this tradition. Barth's theory, not philosophic but religious, has been valuable in rescuing Protestant thought from naturalism and rationalism. The move to restore the emotional nature of religion, one reflected in Peter Marshall and Billy Graham, is modified somewhat by Reinhold Niebuhr.

REINHOLD NIEBUHR

Niebuhr has "socialized" Barth's thought, while still keeping this existentialism religious and Protestant. He starts with the worry that man in the mass is more evil than individual man. (We meet this view in modern social thought, which insists on blaming society for the mistakes of the individual.) Because his theological concerns are dominant, Niebuhr asserts that man's nature is such that he has been traditionally driven between evil and good. On the one hand, man is no more than a child of nature, a child who is compelled by its physical demands and driven by its impulses; on the other hand, man is a spirit who can stand outside nature, life, himself, and the world. As a result of despair, crisis, and anguish over his condition, he has a power that can help him. He can view himself as an object. When he views himself as an object, he realizes that he has two alternatives: faith or sin. Sin results when, having passed through anguish to the point of seeing himself and having examined himself, he decides to devote himself to his self, rather than to God. Man's greatest virtue is voting for God over self-love. Because every encounter with life involves a new crisis and a new examination of the choice between God and self, man can never experience the spontaneous self-giving love that is truly God's. Thus, no human problem is ever soluble, but only approximately so. There are no absolute goods or evils; evil is the result of a particular experience wherein the individual votes, at that time and occasion, for his self. In order to live in a practical and immediate world, Niebuhr places his emphasis in "social gospel." The ethical side of religion is to be stressed. Since the Kingdom of God is not possible in this life, the solution for the individual is to vote, after each crisis of despair and anguish, for his fellow man, rather than for himself. Thus social love is created. The only solution for conflicts between social groups—between labor and employer, for example—is in democracy. As each individual goes through anguish and self-examination and crisis over encounters with the world's experience, each group must also behave in the same way. Such action results in a group love. Through conflict and crisis the groups rise above themselves and see themselves as living objects: when they choose "they" rather than "we," another ethical step has been realized. However, lack of permanence that is found in "essence" is significant. The decision tomorrow is not bound by the principles of that decision today. Each situation is "relative." The only essence or absolute is that the situation will always be "relative." Today's justice may be tomorrow's injustice. Niebuhr stated dramatically:

> Man's capacity for justice makes democracy possible; but man's inclination to injustice makes democracy necessary.

How is the anxiety brought in to man? The cause is the will; man must accept the fact that he is to be an everlasting battleground for deciding to accept anxiety as good, as a sign of living. He can sin in two ways: he can choose self over man and God, or he can refuse to accept anxiety as the will of God.

There is a strong pessimism in Niehbuhr's point of view. There is no progress. Man, overall, can never become better, historically. A single man may become better, but over centuries the race of man is never better. Since no man can win the conflict between reason and nature permanently, every opportunity for good brings in direct proportion a greater possibility for evil. Atomic research brings the possibility of unlimited industrial energy, but also the equal possibility for atomic disaster. The increasing tendency of social, political, and judicial groups to consider each case as unique in nature and as removed from absolute principles is noted in our current life situations.

KARL JASPERS

Jaspers has extended existentialist principles to society. His thesis is that existence cannot be described except by each individual in a concrete situation. Since God is no longer a matter of essence and since there are no absolute principles of mind, heart, and body, man must choose. He is free because man chooses from the self, and not through external dictates. Jaspers drives home the thesis that existence is never complete—as are principles of reason, that man is always in the process of realizing the self. Man is always "on the way." He moves from one crisis to another, each time moving along the road to a clearer understanding of a self that will never be completely understood. Elements of this point of view are visible in *Long Day's Journey into Night* and in the novels of John O'Hara and Salinger. In the existentialist fashion and in man's modern practice, the essence of Nature, God, and the World are rejected as a starting point. Jaspers approaches the program of clarification from the Being of the individual self. Any single man is always burdened with his responsibility for choosing and with the burdens of his decisions. Small wonder at the incidence of mental illness, abnormal social behavior, and suicide. Man is free, however, because no one can choose for him; therefore, he can be bound only by his own decisions. Of course, he must choose.

MARTIN HEIDEGGER

Heidegger's position is important in that he influenced Sartre's literary existentialism. He believes that the world is solely a matter of human concern; man exists in the world, and man's existence as such is that which constitutes the world as having any real significance. The reader should see by now that this assertion is opposed to the tenets of naturalism, one of which asserts, flatly, that the only meaning man can have is that of some unique combination of bits of fundamental matter, all controlled by the God, nature. Man shares this world with other selves like him. Man is concerned with two crises: his encounters with the physical environment and his encounters with a world of communal "existents." Man has three characteristics: he has the fact of being in a physical world; he is a being who is on the way to becoming a greater being through being forced to decide and to be bound by past decisions; and he has the negative quality of being that which can oppose his becoming greater. The qualities that thwart him in his decisions and in a willingness to be bound by his decisions are intellectual curiosity, the tendency to take a "fuzzy view of himself," and a tendency to throw himself on others. Man has an infinite number of choices to make, each requiring a crisis of anguish. In these crises man finds no mind, no spirit, no body. He sees only limitation to himself, and death. In the grim hour of having reduced all consciousness to nothingness, man's will, his driving irrational force, makes a choice, abides by the choice, and realizes that he at least exists.

NIKOLAI BERDYAEV

Berdyaev believes that knowledge is not absolute but obtained through "living." Berdyaev agrees that the claims of science are powerful, but that ethical knowledge is different because of not being about objects and events. A person has the ability to be moral, and he realizes that he is moral when he alone chooses. In order to have morality and ethics, man must go through the crisis of being conscious of himself to himself. Berdyaev makes man encounter experience directly and suffer through to a triumphant knowledge of himself as one who must choose, who does choose, and who is finally willing to abide with his choice.

Berdyaev is like Dostoevsky in insisting that God be justified.

Berdyaev also argues that God is the Creator over that which exists, but God has no power over that which is nonbeing, that which is primeval, that which is called "uncreated" freedom. The fact of uncreated freedom accounts for the dark side of human nature, out of which come both creativeness and destructiveness. Freedom allows for continuing re-creation with God, but also for the rise of evil. What is significant here is that God has no meaning apart from the being—the individual. Thus we are back to the individual as that which lives, exists, that which gives rather than receives meaning. At best, God is the co-creator. Thus, man can conquer naturalism by consistently refusing to choose nature.

Berdyaev is really stating that the creative process is not yet complete. Like the Russian "hero" of Kipling's *The Man Who Was,* he represents a new era yet to come. In a way, modern man is like a relay runner who takes the baton on a course which is always to be run, but a course whose every step means a new creativity. The difference between this relay course and a traditional course is that the runner here receives the baton from a metaphysical level. Each man is conscious of himself as having been created by a creator; this consciousness, directed in at himself, drives him to continue, in himself only, the process of a creation. Because his creativity exists in the consciousness of the individual, he must gain complete freedom for himself. Clinging to an acceptance of God, he decides, in his philosophy, that each man must free himself from external forces. He believes that knowing an "object," as in traditional philosophy and literature, stands in the way of knowing himself as a creator in the continuum of the Creator. Thus, he must oppose all rational systems, even to the extent of making himself an anarchist.

Berdyaev believes that traditional religions, ethics, and socio-logical ideas and ideals enslave man to the outside, keeping his subjective self in chains. Thus, we see here the very seeds of the modern literary existentialists, at the extreme exemplified in the writings of Jean Genet—particularly in *Our Lady of the Flowers*. Such a philosophy, in the hands of a religious person such as Berdyaev, must result in a self-perceived omnipotence.

JACQUES MARITAIN

Maritain's position is quite clear. He admits two types of existentialism. The first is an affirmation of the primacy of existence. Yet, he retains qualities of essentialism because he insists upon making man's mind and understanding supreme. In so doing, he preserves the traditional concepts of the essence of man and of the nature of man. He considers this first position to be the authentic existentialism. The second way also affirms the primacy of existence. This way, which he feels is the current kind, abolishes essence or natures and manifests a complete defeat of intelligibility and intellect. Maritain is of the opinion that this way does not signify anything at all.

Having made his reliance on reason known, Maritain comes as close to existentialism as he will permit himself to come. He distinguishes between a human being as individuality and personality. He is both an individual and a person. As an individual he is related to a community of other individuals as the part is to the whole. Because he is also a person, he is more than a social and political entity. He possesses natural rights, and thus belongs to society as an individual and has higher rights than society as a person. His higher rights involve his relationship with God. Some of his thought appears in Robinson's *The Cardinal, Water of Life,* and *The Big Snow*. His thinking is also evident in Graham Greene's novels, particularly in *The Heart of the Matter, The Man Within,* and *The Power and the Glory.*

PAUL TILLICH

Tillich's *The Courage to Be* contains the great Protestant existential doctrine. Tillich has tried to salvage American Protestantism as Maritain has worked for his Catholic Church. His doctrine is more positive than Maritain's in that he starts with courage as the first sign that man is an ethical being. Courage is the self-affirmation of one's being. Man exists when he has courage to make a choice in a world of opposition of science, destructive emotions, and conflicting concepts. Man has an acute anxiety because he is overcome with the forces arrayed against him, forces that give him a feeling of being annihilated, of death-in-life. He distinguishes anxiety as being of three states: anxiety about fate and death—social; anxiety of guilt and condemnation—spiritual; and anxiety of emptiness and meaninglessness—psychological. To Tillich as theologian, spiritual anxiety is the worst. Existential anxiety can never be removed, but can be a bond of sympathy through communion with other existentialists. The courage "to be" in the person communicates itself to a courage "to be" in other isolated people. Tillich holds the thesis that the only defense against naturalism and romanicism is existentialism. The existentialist strives to preserve the person who is self-affirmative. The concern of existentialism is to defend the individual from objectivization of society, technology, and abstract thought alike.

Two Social Proponents

GABRIEL MARCEL

Marcel's existential thought has certain appeal to this generation. He always stresses the concrete and particular situations, those we see on our TV programs. Existential thinking is threatened by those who would impose abstract rules and principles upon man. Man's self is threatened by bureaucratic societies. The more complex these societies become in a welfare way, the less they contribute to the inner welfare. The important experience in life is to have the individual become conscious of himself as being in action, not as being acted upon. To know others existentially is to become aware of them, not as things, but as people. Here we have the community, communal, and social part of existentialism. Marcel handles the problem of freedom by having the individual look in upon himself and analyze himself. He then becomes aware that he is free for *commitment* or *treason*. This insight involves commitment (fidelity) when the individual binds himself to a specific choice of action. When he makes a choice and is not willing to be bound by his choice, he commits treason—he has not obeyed Polonius' dictum "to thine ownself be true."

MARTIN BUBER

Buber is important as representing one of the finest Jewish minds of the century and as presenting what can be called a Jewish existentialism. Buber states that there is no essence called "I" but only an "I" existing and known in relationship to something else, as "It" or known in relationship to another man called "Thou." Just as music can be analyzed in notes,

verses, and bars, or experienced as a whole piece rather than as
its parts, so can the "I" relate itself to the "It" or the "Thou." In
other words, a living "I" can be related through living by virtue of encounters with things or people. This encounter is associated, of course, with crisis, self-examination, and choice.
Only when the living "I" actually chooses to be related through
living with "It" or "Thou" can the reality of life be revealed to
the "I." The unity of experience can never be defined, but is
known through individual encounters, through action. The
point which is left somewhat ambiguous is whether the
"Thou" means another person, or another part of the person
who is also "I." In Pirandello's drama, particularly *Henry IV*,
any other "IT" or "THOU" would never turn out to be objective because the "I" always looks at things and people in such
a way as to see them as a part of his own real self. What Pirandello saw was that only an insane person could see the real self.
Logically, one would suppose, reversing the direction from essence *to* existence to essence *from* existence would call for reversing the meaning of such terms as "sane" and "insane."

Three Literary Proponents

SÖREN KIERKEGAARD

Kierkegaard stated that any human individual has a vital
concern for himself, for his own salvation, and desires to consider himself as living. He rejects the essentialism that states
that any man as an individual merely represents qualities of
mankind. A man does not want to be slave to an alien idea.
The reader can see this point of view reflected in the dramas
and prose of England's "Angry Young Men," in our "beatniks," and in Kerouac's and Salinger's prose. Man's intellect is

not sufficient to give him a knowledge of himself as living: he cannot define existence. Therefore, states Kierkegaard, man is in crisis: he despairs. He has a burning desire to recognize himself as living, yet his mind fails him. He sees his heart and mind in conflict. Instead of viewing drama on the stage, he creates his own drama of despair. According to the psychological and literary existentialists, crisis and self-examination, the agony of despair, each alleviated by expressed anguish, lead to the disclosure of the individual as living, as existent, as confirming his self to himself. What happens, further, is that the individual is trapped by an intellect that cannot handle all possible judgments: the intellect is denied, by an effort of will. In short, by conviction, the individual man wills himself to deny the reasonable part of himself. This denial causes despair. Then comes salvation. Kierkegaard further considers that the individual is not afraid of any one specific danger or event. Until he submerges his reason, which demands that he reflect on life, he is anguished by a multitude of possibilities.

The modern world does afford ground for such consideration. Knowledge has multiplied over the past century at almost geometric progression. The number of impacts the individual sustains is now infinitely greater in the world of objects, concepts, and people. He cannot escape ideas, people, and things. They are thrust at him every day in his formal and informal education. He is literally bewildered by a sheer sorting-out process. All these impacts involve possibilities of judgment and action. If everything is possible, what can be certain? What is true in the world of mathematics, social relationships, and human behavior? What is true is that man can be conscious of himself, a one living body. He starts from his consciousness that he, at least, is here. This is Kierkegaard's position.

From this position of self-examination and crisis come three streams of interpretation; these will be discussed under the names of their foremost exponents. Such a treatment is essential, since there would appear to be contradictory interpretations of some aspects of existentialism—in the same way that there are contradictions in romanticism where nature in one poet's view is good, in another poet's view is beautiful, and in another poet's view is immanent, pantheistic, evil, indifferent, or useful.

JEAN-PAUL SARTRE

Sartre, intrepid, uncompromising, and existentialist *par excellence,* makes no exception to his thesis that "existence precedes essence." The human self has existence, but has no essence or nature. Sartre agrees with Hegel that there is a "Being-in-itself." This statement means that there is an absolute sense of mind, spirit, and body. However, Sartre settles this problem by asserting that this "Being-in-itself" has no life, no existence. But there is a "Being-for-itself." Through crisis this "Being-for-itself" is continually active, trying to escape from itself. This act of trying to escape from itself is called "crisis." This "Being-for-itself" expresses its life principle by the carving out of the "Being-in-itself" all the multiple living and nonliving experience of the world. Sartre creates the world of the physical universe we know out of a passive essence. What Sartre is saying is that there are objective forms apart from the individual (Being-for-itself). These are passive and are given shape and meaning only through the living individual. Cleverly, Sartre does not deny the world of matter, mind, and spirit; but he makes that world passive. He makes existence great at the expense of essence. Existence is that which permits essential Being to be its servant for expression.

Sartre made two fatal errors: he would have had better luck

in denying essence, although being less honest to do so. He can now have no meaning without the essence he must bring to life to affirm Being-for-itself. Furthermore, he finishes by making existence essence, a disastrous step! Too late, he finds that existence has been identified with a part of essence—human nature. Still, Sartre fares no worse than others who have tried to justify existentialism philosophically. There is no logical method available to justify eliminating the essence of man.

Jean-Paul Sartre is a serious would-be philosopher, and he is read by an audience that does not read technical philosophy by such people as Heidegger, Buber, Tillich, Kant, and Hume, among others. He is a public person, teacher, novelist, an escaped prisoner of war, and was a worker for the French Resistance. His atheism has a serious aim. He is not so much concerned, important to note, with proving there is no God as he is insistent that God's existence, even if true, would make no difference:

> What man needs is to find himself again and to understand that nothing can save him from himself, not even a valid proof of the existence of God.

In one sense Sartre must be correct: the proof that God exists can save no one. Man does need to discover himself. Kierkegaard would object and say that such is all very well, but that man will never discover himself unless he understands his own brief and troubled crises against the eternal reality which gave him life. Sartre strikes back by stating that man lives only when he takes responsibility for himself, when he makes his own decisions, and when no value is real unless the individual does the creating. Sartre claims that religions push man's responsibility off onto a God. The religious man, instead of making a decision, hustles off to ask God what the next step is!

The Protestant has a difficult time with Sartre's line of reasoning. Though Martin Luther scorned the authoritarianism and infallibility of the Roman Church and questioned the dependence of the Catholic who must solve every problem by going to the priest, he left an answer: man is more daring when he makes the leap to faith in God; he is more free in his faith than he is when he defies God. But Sartre holds his position tenaciously. He will never surrender his starting point of the individual.

Sartre makes the world of the senses, the world of sense, and the world of sensibility dependent for their very existence on the individual person. Without the conscious choosing, willing, agonizing, and deciding by each person, body, mind, and spirit have no life, no being at all. Since each decision is subject to change in terms of the person making the decision, even the worlds of personality—the worlds of thinking, feeling, and sensing—are real for the one person only. We have here the concept of relativism in literature: a decision is valid for one time and place only, and the truth of the personality with its three parts does not extend any further than each single individual.

What is true is that man must choose, but he cannot expect any aid from external and supernatural forces. When he chooses and abides by his choice, humanity and society are aided because he chooses for the good of himself, hence for the good of all.

JEAN GENET

Himself a depraved person in a traditionally moral sense, Genet raises his condemned people to a position of the elect, to a position of triumph. Berdyaev believed that his creativity, divorced from external values and creeds, could and would lead to transfiguration. He desires to ensure a philosophy which is an

.... end of this world of ours with its enslaving objectifications, religious, moral, social, and philosophical alike.

Rejecting this world, he continues:

Christianity is the revelation of another world, and to make it conform to this world is to betray it.

In a world of externals, such as those already mentioned as "enslaving objectifications," and in his own world of depraved felons of all possible degenerative forms, Genet has taken a parallel course, on a much lower ethical and religious level, with Berdyaev. But the philosophy is the same.

Rejecting the realities of naturalism, Genet turns from such unpalatable truths to make the statement:

a kind of unclean and supernatural transposition displaces the truth. Everything within me turns worshipper.

Genet worships eroticism in its most unpalatable forms, yet his creativity cannot be denied. All we can say is that we are stunned by such a concept of creativity, that we abhor such divinity. Nevertheless, Genet remains as a challenge to man to create more sincerely than he—if the rest of mankind, like himself and Berdyaev, rejects naturalism or other traditional externals. Genet, then, represents the great horror of an existentialism which backs itself with existentialism's weapons and shields.

Review of Existentialism

Much has been said—and necessarily so—about the existential personality. The forms are as varied and as dazzling as those of romanticism: they pervade the life of Western civilization, becoming less pervasive in Continental Europe, but more so in America. We can, easily enough, state the basic positions of the existential theses. First, there are those who do not believe in the intellectual, spiritual, and physical absolutes which have traditionally defined mankind. In the light of tradition, man has conformed to or revolted from the absolutes. These individuals have rejected essentialism from the thesis that the individual will that confirms man as living and existing is the only reality. Feelings of despair, agony, and crisis are the signs that each individual exists. Crisis becomes a way of life for him. Only through an infinite number of crises evolve numerous moments of agonies and choices. His triumph is in his continued confirmation of himself to himself as free. He is bound by no other force than that of choice. He is free to choose. Whatevery choice he makes is correct and good for all. If his freedom of choice leads to suicide, drug addiction, drunkenness, or hysteria, or if his freedom of choice leads him to face the agony of existence, he is a victor because the choice is his, not that of someone else.

The second thesis of existentialism is that which leads to the divided self. In such a position, the existentialist admits the reality of such experience as natural forces as impersonal, the world of intellect as externally powerful, and a world of spirit which persists in obtruding itself on the consciousness and the subconsciousness of man. Cutting across the overt and the more subtle reactions to the grim reality these individuals reject is the invariable split among the parts of the human personality—mind, heart, and body. The external self looks outward as a seeker of externals; the inner self seeks reunion with the outer self, but only on its own terms of rejecting any absolute other than itself. All that we have said falls into these two main streams. However, as we have seen, there are unique differences and interpretations. In any case, agony, suffering, pain, despair, choice, and freedom are experienced when they yield to the individual the experience of living, existing.

There is no question that the majority is in the essential tradition. Can there really be an existentialist, we ask? There is no question that for a time, however brief, any person can have a physical state where there is no such experience as external reality. Under the influences of an anesthetic, during his sleep, when he is dead drunk, when he is under the influence of drugs, and when he is insane, he can be without an experience of absolute values. He can be suspended from the world of reality when he is in a world of hysteria. Now, unless the writer is suggesting these states as an escape from reality, he does not deny the world reality, but he challenges the meaning of the world of reality. His challenge will then act so as to put man in a state where he is free from a world he cannot face, or a world he does not want to face.

We can take another position. We can say that what we have known as the worlds of mind, spirit, and body are not real at all. As tradition they have been imposed in the name of mankind on individuals. The human being can and must eliminate these ideas of reality. The elimination is best accomplished by acts of willing. Through agony, despair, and distress at cutting ourselves off from all that consciousness—as tradition—has imposed on us, we can be free individuals who choose. Each movement that turns us toward external reality is, in reality, crisis. To deny a world, sometimes an attractive world, sometimes a terrible world, is to demand a never-ceasing courage. Pushing this thesis far enough, we can see that the exponent of this form of positive existentialism considers that the traditional world was one of illusion. The staunch existentialist will regard his painful experiences as the necessary steps to the vision of the only reality, the self, as existing and totally and comprehensively so.

So strong is this existential faith that its adherents will agree that when the act of loving is necessary to confirm an individual's self as existing, the object of his loving may have to be destroyed. One of the most magnificent examples of existentialistic thought comes in a great play which ultimately refutes existentialism: Christopher Fry's *The Lady's Not For Burning*. Thomas Mendip, a discharged soldier, angrily demands to be hanged: he cannot stand the world of traditional values. Against his will, Thomas meets and is attracted to—also against his will—the beautiful Jennet who loves the world, although she is aware of its frustrating nature. Not being dishonest to himself, Thomas does not want to accept the world as essential; not being one of the existentialists who will "will to love" at the expense of destroying the one loved, Thomas would rather die. At the end of the play Thomas gives in to the world of experience, with reluctance. Not liking his personal self any better, he planned to be extinguished. However, he has saved himself by being able to achieve enough self-fulfillment through Jennet who is staunchly in the world outside. Jennet, unwittingly, proves to be an existential analyst. Fry, implicitly, makes the point that Jennet is the force toward which his restoration to the real self is oriented. Perhaps the real question for every man today is whether that personal self that the existentialist sees can ever be considered a real self. Whatever Thomas sees as a result of his dislike of the real world is not sufficiently horrible to make him desire to spend a lifetime with his personal self. Does the existentialist who commits suicide—or who otherwise destroys his personality by artificial means—do so because he cannot entirely conquer the world of traditional values? Does he do so because the vision of the self without the world seems too frightening to bear? Does he do so because he cannot recommit himself to a world of essence he has rejected?

The Challenge of Science

The philosopher, however, faces the formidable challenge of science, and yet science, with its impacts, forces the existentialist to renew his struggles and to intensify his insistence on making the self a matter of primacy.

We have entered a new world through economic and social change. In passing through the present transitional period, we are going to learn—to be told—what life is going to do. We are finding out that time and space are not separable but are working together, in a living fashion, to shape all matter from a common genesis. No longer can we isolate ourselves from things and view them from the outside. In the eyes of scientists we are nothing more than evolution which has become conscious of itself. Organically one, we are going to have increasing difficulty in dividing reality up into physical, moral, and spiritual realities. Man is not the center of the universe: he is the sign which indicates the last production of evolution; he is the most complicated, the most subtle, and the finest layer, so far, of the layers of earth. Man is conscious of being threatened by a futility at viewing the nature of an expanding universe: he is overwhelmed with the expanse of space. The vast expansion of numbers and the infinite extension of time frighten and overwhelm man. We realize, with fear, that our ancestors who established what we know of man as traditional did not realize the nature of the world in which they lived and for which they made their standards, those binding on themselves and those binding on us. Must we toss them aside? More terrible than anything else, we seem to have, now, the gift of foresight. We are being made sick, sick to death.

We have the anguish of being shut in. We are hemmed in by time and space. If man is the last and most complex force in the world, and if that man now has the gift of foresight, that which our ancestors did not have, are we near the end? Can there be a tomorrow? If all of man's thought and moral stature have moved him toward the end of his evolutionary cycle, why should he, knowing that, move toward his own annihilation? Man drives on, for the most part, only when he believes that he can succeed.

The dangers that can result from the fear of being shut in, limited, and anxious are those of isolation, discouragement, and the will to create a personal universe. These have been shown to exist with existentialism.

If science cannot promise man a logical or an emotionally satisfying way of meeting a universe incredibly large and enduring, she can show man that he has fewer chances of survival on any terms in committing himself to disorder, failure, intellectual and spiritual decomposition, solitude, anxiety, and despair. He can live with hope and love if he is great enough to love the entire universe as he would love great art, poetry, and music. Reality is not too much for a man to bear if he will expand his scope of love and deepen his willingness to look to the great nature in which he is an evolving part. The consciousness of love is itself an evolutionary factor. Since the consciousness of matter has provided a consciousness of love, and since that love, in descending degrees, is a part of the world of animal life, a greater articulation and scope should evolve with a greater rate of evolution: man's capacity for loving and for recognizing what he is loving should increase and improve. Man has been shocked to make nature God herself. The recent statements of the scientific point of view make nature yet God but not impersonal. While maintaining the all-pervading force of the elemental particles of matter as the constituents of all the world of life and nonlife, of all ideas, emotions, and concrete objects, science indicates that the energy form of the basic particles is as much responsible for the power of love as for the power of any natural manifestation. Even though we were not to equate our personal God with the God that is nature, the feeling and response of love are the same. Love is as "real" sensation-wise to man in naturalism as in any traditional form of religion.

Can science object to man's controlling himself through his unique religious manifestations and creeds? Apparently not! The combinations of particles that would give the scientist manifestations of matter and energy as real would also admit the reality of the religious impulse. He would probably apply the same criteria to the survival of particular religious expressions as he would to any other problem of survival. Those most fit for the total evolution of man as inside matter itself would survive in the light of the best advantages for that time and space in the world.

The extent of World War II brought home as real experiences the isolation and despair felt by Germany after World War I. Imprisonment, torture, and mass annihilations involved man in religious, economic, political, and social concerns about the individual and his place in this world. We have noted in earlier comments that science is posing all men a problem. She gives the answer to man's relationship to his world of matter, and does so whether or not he desires the answer. The experiences of World War II are real ones, and were real as personal experiences to the writers.

Social conflicts with minority groups, the vastly increased number of objective facts, and an incredible multiplication of personal and objective impacts—as ideas and events—impinge on an individual whose past experiences do not seem to enable him to meet the incredible speed of modern communications. Not only must the individual place himself on trial to himself, but also involve himself in a society which places its individual members and itself under a self-scrutiny. Traditionally, he could avoid his own society in exchange for religion, growing African violets, building his own rock garden, erecting metal railings around his house, and in joining exclusive social, political, and religious organizations.

Man recoils from a society to which he must conform. He is forced, physically, to conform. Today all workers work in groups. Research is done by the group. Teaching is being done by teams. There seems no way out for the individual. As much as he hates his self, he finds the society into which he is forced little better. Anxiety today can spring from two sources: man has lost his footing in the world of external reality, or he finds his footing in the world of physical and intellectual impact he detests and would avoid. If man cannot create—or restore—a world of essential values, his best solution is to commit himself, irrevocably, to his most moral oath.

The existentialists, in devoting themselves to this most moral oath must struggle against loss of identity.

Courage to Be "One"

The existentialist struggles against any form of dehumanization. According to the existential view, the major task of every individual is to be himself. The determined, authentic individual will not accept a directive from any external force. The source the individual has of security against the loss of spiritual meaning, moral disintegration, or the threat of annihilation, can come from no other person, or source, except the individual himself. The individual is "saved" by this courage alone, as Tillich urges. However, the courage comes from outside the individual and can come in one of two ways: the courage can be supplied by doctor, nurse, or other party who has no anxiety, no choice to make, and no freedom to affirm. If such is the case, there is a fatal contradiction, for the individual must provide his own insight and courage. In this case, there is bad art. In the other case, the individual is saved by a doctor, nurse, or by someone else who has won a personal triumph through anxiety, courage to choose, and the proper use of freedom to commit himself to fidelity in himself and in others. This solution is a sounder solution, but there is a serious dramatic problem in the traditional sense of having two heroes and no villains, or all villains and no heroes.

At this point one must turn to the literary scene where existentialism has made heavy impact.

Chapter 4

Naturalism, Romanticism, and Existentialism: The Literary Sense

Introductory

In reviewing many works, we shall indicate the point at which we believe that we can call some writers "existential," the point where we can call some works "existentialistic," and the point where we believe that we have a thoroughgoing existentialist. We have the "true-blue" existentialist in Sartre. There is no question of his carrying the full equipment, all of the basic qualities. Genet is also a bona fide existentialist. Albee and Beckett carry impressive credentials. Anouilh is eclectic; he carries, as do the works of Camus and Giraudoux, notable existential qualities. We shall review the works of many authors in Continental Europe, England, and the United States.

The first procedure will be to note the basic qualities of naturalism, existentialism, and romanticism. We shall point out the signs which differentiate—"markers"—one philosophy from another.

Comparative Listing of Naturalistic, Romantic and Existential Qualities in a Literary Sense.

Naturalism

1. Life is recorded and observed, not evaluated (Hemingway, Steinbeck, Flaubert).

2. Moral "absolutes" such as "truth," "justice," "kindness," "mercy," and "charity," are only terms of no more or less importance than the names of chemical products.

3. The literature shows lack of interest in, or indifference to, character.

4. The literature insists on showing the seamy side of life.

5. The literature tries to evoke sensations for their own sakes.

6. The literature emphasizes the pessimistic view of man, man as comic.

7. Naturalism denies free will: the determinism rests in the rigor of mathematical laws and in the relentlessness of blind biological principles.

8. Naturalism makes no critical evaluations of the characters as furnishing grounds for the imagination. The characters are placed in real life situations. They are viewed with the analytical and objective views of the scientist.

9. Man is always debased. He is made nontheistic and non-rationalistic.

10. Man is always trapped by social forces (*An American Tragedy*). He is always pulled down from aspirations and lofty visions by people who are not as good as he is. The lion loses to the jackal.

11. Naturalism steers away from that which is naturally lyrical and poetic. Such must be the case because that poetic frame of mind needs the synthesis of body, mind, and heart.

12. The prose style is below dramatic level: flat, bare of imagery, lacking rich ambiguity, and stuffed, on the other hand, with myriads of details. Colorful metaphor is anathema.

13. Naturalism equates man with the basic particles of matter. Man is simply a unique arrangement of basic elements common to both living and nonliving matter. Constant motion is the only absolute accepted as to matter. When naturalism equates man with matter, the equation is worked in such a way as to stress that which is sordid, ugly, vicious, and primitive.

14. Naturalism, based on the common unit of the atom and its parts or the molecule in motion, is usually concerned with the common class, with social and industrial conflicts, and holds in contempt traditional institutions of church, state, family, and ethics—as absolute.

15. The romanticist placed gods or God in nature as immanent or pantheistic; the rationalists placed matter in the mind; the romanticist also placed matter in the heart, but the believers in naturalism place mind and spirit in matter. Thus, in naturalism, nature herself is God, not God in nature.

16. The romanticist tries to make the common "uncommon," the rationalist distinguishes between the common and the uncommon; the believer in naturalism keeps the common very "common."

17. From a religious point of view, the believer in naturalism sees the entire universe as entirely impersonal. What happens, happens because of natural law—physical and biological. Man is in debt to nature for the very basic matter of which he is composed; he is her slave; nature is all-powerful and all-controlling.

18. What man considers "right" and "wrong" are only steps in a blind evolutionary force. Man is but a fraction of a second in a vast order of evolution; a man is even less than a billionth of a second in the time order of evolution.

19. Man is controlled by chance, the random but average force of molecules and atoms, as relentlessly as any other force is controlled.

20. Naturalism reveals that man's mind evolved, as did all other forms, from the most primitive and undifferentiated form of matter. The mind has evolved through time, becoming more complex, more cognitive. However, there is no proof that the evolutionary process that brings about the development—or evolution—of the mind is different from the evolutionary process that develops other living forms. The mind depends almost entirely on the complete nervous system.

21. Psychology today stresses that man's intelligence reveals no faculty that can possibly be called divine. Man may have reason, but he prefers to live with irrationality. He uses his reason for rationalization. His so-called metaphysical concepts and religious proclivities are little more than dreams, fancies, fantasies, and wishful thinking.

22. Religion has been accepted not because of its truth, but because of its falsity. The real world is too cold to face; therefore, people have compensated reality through creating unreal but warmer worlds.

23. Naturalism suggests that men have a religion without God. The only god to which we can turn is nature. She suggests that we learn more about the truths of human nature, and that we make our adjustment as individuals with a group.

24. Naturalism has interesting aspects on the psychological level. All dreams are attempts to fulfill what has been frustrated by real nature. Thus man realizes through dreams what consciousness will not permit.

25. Man does have a religious nature, but that nature is one that equates goodness with family and community approval. Man suffers guilt when he displeases family and community mores and morals. He would rather feel good than be correct.

26. The ego is that part of man which tries to achieve a balance between man's irrationality and nature's rationality.

27. The id provides drives that try to have man act as though he were impervious to the order of nature and reason.

28. Certain aspects of surrealism lend themselves to naturalism; some to romanticism, and some to existentialism. The movement is almost exclusively artistic and literary. The members of this group believe that what we know in our everyday conscious level is arbitrarily constructed by the mind and determined through custom. Surrealists also believe that the subconscious levels bring us closer to the primitivism that was at home with nature as she really is.

29. These are the main principles of naturalism: *Natura sive deus*—nature is absolute. "I perceive; therefore, I am." This perceiving, however, is not consciousness, but the direct physical world, and the scientific aspects of psychology.

Romanticism

1. The romanticist believes that the world of imagination is the world of eternity.

2. The romanticist looks ahead to the future, back to the past, and, generally, loathes the present.

3. The romanticist opposes, vigorously, institutions and organized dogma.

4. Whereas the Christian and Mohammedan have God inside the world as immanent and outside the world as transcendent; whereas the deist has God outside the world as transcendent only; the romanticist has God entirely inside the world of matter as immanent, thus making all forms of matter equally divine.

5. The romanticist is uniquely lacking a sense of humor, and is usually devoid of the comic impulse.

6. The romanticist is heavily oriented toward a sensuous reaction to the world of experience.

7. The romanticist is strongly intuitive in holding that the great truths come to mind independent of the intellectual core of man.

8. The romanticist is quite pantheistic when his emphasis is not on the immanent. The difference is that in pantheism, there are many gods; in immanence, God is inside nature and not transcendent.

9. The romanticist is seldom specific in his ideas; the volitional aspects are normally overpowering, but he is quite concrete in applying his ideas to sensory terms.

10. The true romanticist is seldom sensual—although he may be sensuous.

11. The romanticist is a defender of human freedom in terms of the individual.

12. The romanticist leans heavily on the interpretation of physical nature—which ranges from nature as friendly, beautiful, good, and religious, to nature as unfriendly, hostile, indifferent, and evil.

13. The romanticist (Hopkins, for example) may also believe that nature exists solely as a highway to God.

14. The romanticist is essentially introverted.

15. The romanticist is essentially anti-intellectual in developing support for his own abstractions; example—Shelley.

16. The romanticist, because of his total dependence on sensory material for elucidation and because of an essential pantheism and belief in immanence, is inclusive rather than exclusive.

17. The romanticist is inclined to assert that innocence and virtue are equated in the child; maturity brings knowledge of evil.

18. Romanticism, in some forms, lends itself to a primitivism in asserting that man's total personality should respond purely to instinct.

19. The romanticist always hearkens to an inner demand to devote oneself to the world of spirit. The world of spirit equates with and reveals imagination—which the romanticist further equates with God.

20. Finally, the romanticist believes that he alone is able to grasp Plato's Ideal Forms as reality and to use the imagination to create visible shapes of these forms and realities.

21. The function of the artist and writer is to discover the real world as originally experienced and felt.

22. Literature is that creativity which clarifies and manifests the impressions, the emotions, the institutions, and the attitudes of the artist.

23. Art and literature have their basic foundations and origins in the experiences and feelings of the creators of the interests of the human soul.

24. True literature is that which is a statement of the soul of the artist and writer, not of objects outside the soul; although these objects may be used to reflect or interpret the inner being.

25. The writer has no responsibility concerning the world, other than that of pleasing himself.

26. Beauty is most closely equated with passionate intensity and conviction, that which is truly original, and that which is entirely sincere.

27. The romantic statement exists as true and complete in itself, not open to question.

28. *Ago, ergo sum;* I act; therefore I am. By "act" here we mean volition, willing, conation, and the emotive aspects of man's nature.

Existentialism

1. Existentialism opposes any absolutes; thus, naturalism's "I perceive; therefore, I am," is rejected as accepting the binding control of nature's laws.

   Rationalism's *Cogito; ergo sum*—"I think; therefore, I am"—is not acceptable. Existentialism rejects this statement since the individual would have to derive his entire existence from the essence of thought, a faculty outside and beyond man.

   Romanticism's "I will; therefore, I am" is equally objectionable. The existentialist who is atheistic will accept no God. The existentialist who is non-atheistic will not accept a God in nature as immanent.

2. The existentialist starts with experience first: he exists; because he exists, he thinks; he feels; he perceives. *Nihil sive deus*—existence before essence.

3. The existentialist commences with the "feel" of human existence, with the human restricted to his "personal" existence.

4. Every individual faces the fact of living; he faces this existence through his own consciousness.

5. Our feeling, our state, our existence is one of dread, and anxiety.

6. The use of fear usually is in the context of a material object: man, examinations, and the threat of rain, for example.

7. With dread we are thrown into states. We have the predicate noun situation as "dread of choosing," "dread of facing," "dread of feeling," "dread of making." We avoid the object; thus, what we dread is nothing. Equating dread with the act, when we pull the acting, choosing, willing, or facing to the left-hand side of the equation, we have nothing.

8. When the existentialist is no longer conscious of himself as being, he feels that he is nothing.

9. The existentialist denies that there are absolute truths in religion.

10. The existentialist denies that there are absolute truths in ethics.

11. The existentialist starts with his own personal philosophy; he ends with his own personal philosophy.

12. Because his deepest emotive states are from his own personal histories and because they are his personal histories, he will go to any length to provide the material for such historicity —within himself.

13. The existentialist, because he is filled with foreboding concerning the predicament of himself as man, is also filled with foreboding for the predicament of other men.

14. The existentialist rejects the ideal thinker in Plato's world; he rejects the social individual postulated by Dewey; and he has little regard for Aristotle's concept of man. He opposes both authoritarianism and certitude.

15. The existentialist cares only for the specific man, the man of flesh, bone, and self-ness. Thus, the existentialist is interested only in the individual and in the unique existence of a particular person, himself. This person, however, is never free from passion and suffering.

16. The existentialist must always start with his "being" because the Being is his own.

17. The existentialist reasons as follows:
    a. To exist is to be caught.
    b. To be caught is to be caught in existence.
    c. To be caught in his own existence is a predicament.
    d. Man is free because he is the origin of his own "ing" states.
    e. Because each man knows that he is free and that he is

the origin of his own having, possessing, creating, and existing, he is in anguish, pain, and dread.

  f. Nearly all people try to deny their own freedom. They make believe that they are not free; therefore, they bind themselves with moral bonds and bounds which they claim are higher than their wills.

    i. But each man is isolated, alone with his own freedom.

    ii. No other person or agency—except time—can take this burden, this freedom from him.

    iii. Not to bind himself to these truths is to be dishonest in all respects.

    iv. The only alternative to despairing at the crushing weight of reality is to create, to possess, and to exist; but expressed as creating, possessing, and existing.

    v. Man should never fool himself with any hope of future success.

    vi. Life's meaning is to be derived by the individual from a continual series of engagements and commitments of choosing and acting, the gerundial state.

18. Whence do we derive this agony, despair, and anguish?

  a. Reality has its meaning—assuredly—only with the mind of a man, but not all reality is in the consciousness of "awareness-of-Beingness."

  b. The outer or perceptual world exists as real.

  c. The existentialist directs himself toward physical objects, keeping in mind that other people are physical objects.

  d. The existentialist desires to achieve unity, complete synthesis, and can do so only with the reality not in his human consciousness.

  e. He is driven to identify himself with all reality. He refuses to give up the central thesis of his "for-itself" as human consciousness. He must yield on the point of human consciousness to achieve unity—wholeness.

f. He is caught in a terrible contradiction. To be unified —synthesized—and made whole with reality, he will have to look to the tradition which has always made each man partake of the common essence of man. If he surrenders all mental phenomena and human consciousness, he is threatened with the specter of naturalism, his greatest foe.

g. Thus, human existence is replete with lack of fulfillment, emptiness, and frustration.

h. As individuals we are free; we can be free, and we can stay free. Coming from the bitterness of an anguish we know will always be ours, because we can never be made one with all reality, is the concept that we have liberty.

i. Each man knows that he must always choose his consciousness—Awareness-of-Beingness—above being unified with reality. He is free to despair; he is free to choose. Since he is cut off from God, from men who are essentialists, and from all reality except his own self-consciousness, he must make all the choices. There are many possibilities from which he can and must choose. He has no jury outside himself. Thus, he is completely free. He is free to despair because he must do all the choosing with no criteria as objective to aid him in his choosing. Thus, he must despair because all reality throws itself against him. He can only make his choice and despair as to its possible effectiveness.

19. The existentialist believes that belief is consciousness of choosing. Thus, there is no belief apart from the choosing, willing and acting individual.

20. Sartre's statement is significant. Choice is always possible, but what is not possible is not to choose. I can always choose, but I ought to know that if I do not choose, I am still choosing—in terms of my own consciousness.

21. Whether the existentialists are Christian or atheistic, or some other non-Christian, as Hebraic or Mohammedan, they all

believe that existence comes before essence. Subjectivity is the starting point.

22. The word "atheistic" is not significant as used, because the atheistic existentialist does not consider that God's reality is significant. Because each man is just what he is by way of acting, choosing, and willing, he has only his own law. Thus, God, if existent, would not enter the picture.

23. When he fulfills himself, he exists. This fulfilling can come only through the agony of choices which uphold his own self-consciousness. When a man no longer has the agony, there is no longer Being, but entire Nothingness—or entire object.

24. The conviction of making choices is never one of reason, only one of intense passion: human existence is no more than passion.

25. The existentialist must make every individual aware of his own nature. He must perceive and suffer the terrible weight of responsibility upon himself.

26. What counts as real is the individual's inner response to a situation which he has experienced.

27. Man's emotional outlook on the world of experience is formed by mental associations. The thing seen or imagined stands for the person who may own the thing, or has owned the thing.

28. The existentialist, part tragic and part comic, produces and acts in his own melodramas.

29. There is no set personality that is given to man just because he is man; his consciousness of self is entirely personal.

30. When man stands out against reality, defending his choice with respect to other choices he might have made, he finds his meaning in the negations he has created through ignoring the rest of reality.

31. One assertion creates its opposite; such is true of love. The

assertion of love is one that devours and brings, as nearly concurrently, hate.

32. Man is driven by the urge for creating, possessing, and existing—almost in that order.

33. When man becomes aware of the world in a sensory fashion, this awareness of his body gives him a feeling of nausea.

34. The marked sexual tones of the literature are, more often than not, results of needs and drives which use sexuality for a method of expression.

35. The greatest anxiety for the existentialist must be that his response in any specific situation can never be a total response in the light of his entire seeking, lacking, and needing.

36. The existentialist must face the specter of bad faith: he may convince himself that he can stop being what he is to be something else.

37. When we imagine, or when we are imagining, the consciousness seeks an object not through the object as in perceiving, but through an image or images of the object. When we say "image" of the object, we do not mean a physical mirrored reflection. We do mean that the object furnishes grounds for the imagination, but not in a specific, objective way.

38. The dramatic sensations and sensory responses with sex give meaning to the individual's affirmation or negation. He is left with a strong conscious reaction which gives him the feeling of controlling the world in terms of himself. He achieves this feeling of completeness within himself when he is conscious of himself as the "subject" which controls the "other" (individual) without himself being controlled or possessed by any external person or force. That is, as long as he keeps himself, the subject, free from control by the "other," the object, he stands outside of—and free from—any order except his own.

39. Because in every existential self there beats the pulsing con-

sciousness to be creating, possessing, and existing, the sexual relationships, the violence against the person, and the defiance of the law are common to existential literature.

40. Literary materials will reflect the problems in and of consciousness. The existentialist considers two kinds of consciousness: reflective and nonreflective. The reflective variety is that which reflects upon the consciousness already reflected upon. In nonreflective consciousness, we have the "for Itself" studying a conscious with a structure of emotional or emotive states.

41. The novel is not about things but is about the consciousness of things, insofar as the reality is involved in the behavior of specific individuals, who must be free. They must not be determined by any traditional absolutes such as genetics, rigid environment, and religious determinations.

42. Objects can *be* because they have only externals to appear to us; but minds *become,* perhaps as flowing streams of consciousness, and through transformations of reality. A novel must not annihilate the mind of the character. Sartre believes that the author must not be omniscient; he must not make the judgment.

43. Novelists should have a keen sense of time as flowing; if the judgment is absolute or omnipotent, time stops. What happens if time breaks down? Then there is no flow. Consciousness flows from individuals in their creating, possessing, and existing through time.

44. The novelist should use time in such a way as to furnish a series of conflicts or crises for the characters. But he must furnish these blocks or frustrations in such a way as to have the characters conscious that they are eating up future moments of their lives because of the problems they have to set up or to solve, as the case may be. The story must flow from people in real situations. People in real situations know that the price of living through experience is that of gobbling up moments of the fleeting future, in time that is available to them.

45. Man is absurd, but we must not start with that position. That position must emerge from characters in their creating, possessing, and existing. This position is revealed with a great light—intuition or insight. Man is absurd because he cannot fuse "awareness of Being-ness" with "Being-in-Itself," as God could do.

46. Man is absurd. He could escape his agony by suicide, alcoholism, protracted narcotic states, and other abnormal acts against human existence, but he avoids these. He prefers to live with his consciousness—certain only of uncertainty. He learns to accept and to live with the fact of death. He equates his constant negation as a death, or as reduction to nothingness. He faces the certainty of having each actualized future as a "present" equal to the death of time, the death of experience, and the death that follows—as failure—any attempt for human consciousness to transcend "seeking reality" and "fusing with reality."

47. The only purpose that a novel should have is to have none. We could have written another novel as well as this one. There was no inner compulsion to state absolute truths. This was an experience that could have been any other experience. This was a day like any other old day could have been.

48. Some existential writers employ sentences that are self-contained and that follow each other in such a way as to annihilate the state before and introduce a new state. If the author, like Camus, places the narrative in the present tense, there is an agonizing sense of alienation. We are tearing experience and life from the future, actualizing a large series of the immediate futures. Because each sentence reveals death and life, then we agonize more of the greater number of isolations. We are continually moving to death in the framework of presents slipping into the pasts, but we are also moving, alone, to the future. We have isolation no matter which way we look. Either the past pushes man ahead to death and rebirth, or the future leans in on us as we stand out against experience.

49. A key to much of the existential mind is the deep-seated realization that consciousness is always a future matter. Why must this statement be true? Consciousness is "lack," "need," "awareness-of-Being-ness," or "for-Itself." There is a need for continual devouring, eating up. But these bites are like the sentences, one destroyed, another created, and any projection eats into the future. That is the only direction for consciousness.

50. In seeking for meaning in man, we cannot lose sight of the fact that the geometrical statement that the whole is equal to the sum of its parts will not work in existential philosophy. The individual is not the sum of his parts. He does not have them all—they are always in the future with his projected consciousness. Man is what he is and what he is going to do, what he cannot do, or what he could have done.

51. Because of what I am, as an existentialist, I cannot stop time, except through death, suicide, insanity, alcoholism, or narcotics addiction. I must know that there is a perceptual world of objects to which I must address—and seek from myself—myself, and such can be done only in a time with a future.

Chapter 5

First Modern Existentialists: Literary Sense

Sören Kierkegaard

In considering the art of Kierkegaard (1813–1855), we look to the irrational stream of existentialism and to the Christian elements. We are interested, because much of Western literature and art is in the Christian and Jewish tradition—not the art as such, but the viewing of the art. Kierkegaard realized that the individual must be saved as an individual, saved from evolution, saved from gathering religious lethargy, and saved from the age of the machine. He must withdraw from the absolutes which were now being found in physical science, mathematics, and group ideologies. Thus, Kierkegaard started with each single man: each man has responsibility; he suffers; he is not complex; he must die since he is not immortal. He avoided considering what makes a man "a man" from the point of view of starting with the qualities of man.

Kierkegaard pointed out that no one is more interested in a single man than the single man himself. Because Kierkegaard was an intensely religious person, he viewed the individual—

Joe Jones—as considering his soul as more important than his temporal existence. If man is to exist, he must do so as a moral single person who has to satisfy God. Such a man has dread, alienation, and despair because, cut off from essentials as outside rules, he must pass through a vast number of seconds and minutes, making a decision with respect to God. Every man despairs because he cannot guarantee that he has made the correct decision. Furthermore, the decision of S_1 (where S is a unit of time and the numbers represent choices, numerically named) cannot determine S_2, S_3, and so on through all futurity. (We must stop long enough to suggest to the reader that even if we may not have sound theology here, there is the basis for good drama and literature. Each coming choice must be dramatic as "surprise," since the current experience has value only in itself, not having itself bound to past seconds.)

For Kierkegaard the best position for launching a meaningful life in terms of the self is to start with "I live." He lives; therefore he may think, act, and feel. One does not discuss experience; one does not reflect about experience; one should live. One should not talk about Christ; one should live Christ. A man does not think about poetry; he lives poetry. When an individual makes up rules, he makes an error. His living and his experience are rules. One is transformed inwardly from handling the individual experience.

Man must be identifiable as an individual. He must not be an average man, an average student, an average novelist, or an average Christian. He must not be just like any other member of a group. He is not a typical factory worker, nor a typical "suburbanite," but an individual unique because of his individualism. He must not be one who will believe that "The State Is God" (as Fichte stated).

From Kierkegaard the majority of existential thinking has

accepted the concept of "dread" as opposed to fear. "Anxiety" is another acceptable word for the state of "dread." "Dread," as ordinarily used, is much more negative than Kierkegaard's concept. As we have indicated earlier, "dread" and "anxiety" are states which do not demand nor take an object. We "fear" something or things.

Fyodor Dostoevsky

Dostoevsky (1822–81) is here considered with respect to his existential qualities; he possessed several. We are not concerned with his stature, although his authorship is indeed formidable. We know that he created his own huge and mysterious worlds. We know that his realms are those filled with terror. We know that he also had the existential quality of analysis of his own guilt. His works have enough of the sordid and seamy material of naturalism, but his reality is equally of the stuff of the existential mind. He took the raw material of life in action. Whether his psychology is more Freudian than existential is a matter of debate, but he exhibits much of the existential psychic process. This Russian writer experienced, at first hand, the agony, despair, and isolation of being exiled four years in Siberia. Gambler, debtor, revolutionist, poverty-stricken individual, he acquired sufficient experience of and from life well before he started his great literary career.

His literary qualities include the use of realistic detail, employment of romantic morbidness, the view of nature as vast and frightening, the habitual obsession with evil and redemption, and the display of a love for humanity. He lived with primitive, brutal, callous, and depraved souls in Siberia. He had tender moments of compassion, but came to regard man as somewhat of a demon, completely beyond reason.

The author's *Crime and Punishment* is existential. Man here stands out; he is violent; he demands his own punishment. The central figure, Raskolnikov, is an intellectualist. He propounds a theory through which he shall live in the light of his morality. He shall be his own code. His crime is scarcely heroic: an old pawnbroker is killed. Here we come to a split in personality: the break between the intellectual and the irrational. Raskolnikov cannot know his irrational self which now strikes. The unconsciousness now imposes such responses as horror and terror at his murder. The intellect tries to rationalize away the murder, but not successfully. Why has he killed? To establish his own law, to give himself meaning to himself!

His intellect does not always serve him kindly; he realizes that the emphasis on volition and will only is alienating in two ways: from society, but, more significantly, from himself. He has that split personality we have been discussing throughout our treatment of the pre-existentialists. Having no significant feelings about himself, he kills in order to prove himself to himself. Facing nothingness, he tries to fill up the void with actions, acting. The acting is antisocial, nonconventional.

Dostoevsky's heroes are ambivalent in ranging from inhumanity to great compassion. Irrespective of how he views the universe, Raskolnikov has a tender compassion and pity for others. As his trials continue, the hero is torn between a need to live and a need to die. Which choice will give him the greatest impact about himself to himself? The existential quality of affirming himself in the presence of the negation is strong in Dostoevsky. Facing the fact of death, he affirms, as the author did when they were about to shoot him for his revolt. Thus,

Raskolnikov, debating on death, affirms the value of life. He finally confesses and undergoes his trial. He does so through his own will. At the point of being able to escape, he stands out, finally, to accept his own guilt.

Dostoevsky's art is a fascinating blend of the imagination, the world of dreams and fantasies. What brings the subject away from insanity is ability never to stray too far away from that which is real.

Nevertheless, we do have problems. Before Raskolnikov murders the pawnbroker, he has a long and frightful dream. In the dream, imagination, fantasy, and reality are interwoven so that when he awakens he is unaware that he is acting out a fantasy, but quite aware that he is going to kill the victim. His powerful imagination identifies in his body and its sensations the nature of what the victim will experience and suffer. How does he know that he will kill the old lady? The stuff of consciousness, a flow of fantasy, imagination, and perceptual reality give him such information, and do so irrationally. We have a strong existential fact here. The consciousness of her death is so strong that he feels himself the executed, rather than the executioner. He has experienced becoming an object, rather than remaining subject. The entire story will center on the problem of how he can keep himself as consumer, rather than as consumed. He finally surrenders. The Freudian notes are a little too strong for the Sartrian psychoanalyst. We have something that we cannot measure, that we have to accept as absolute. But what existentialist will accept any fact as absolute, particularly when the fact is the ineffability of both id and superego? (Perhaps Genet!)

André Gide

In considering André Gide, novelist (1869–1951), we have a French Protestant in conflict with his desire to taste the more lively aspects of life. His revolt took the course of freedom from parental and other social ties, sexual unconventionality, a frank and nonhypocritical way of meeting experience, and a private and bizarre morality. Gide, mellowing somewhat, would never accept orthodox religion. He had much of the Renaissance spirit within him. With a will as strong as Luther's, with an influence on him from the Bible as strong as any early Puritan's, Gide also brought a pagan spirit worthy of a Herrick or Donne in their earlier days. However, Gide went well beyond their pagan spirit to out-devil the devil. Compared to the indictments which sent Socrates to his death as a corrupter of youth, Socrates' alleged offenses must be considered tepid indeed when put next to the incitements and corruptions Gide offered to youth in his long life.

Gide encouraged the revolt against rational and literary values. Not only did he encourage the revolt against, but also urged the negation of that traditional world of values prior to 1916. He supported Dada. (Dadaism was a revolt in poetry and painting formulated during World War I. Its theses were that all social conventions must go; the individual could do no wrong if he did not write traditionally; one must behave outrageously in public. Complete anarchy must reign. The movement finally collapsed from its own excesses in 1926. The existential qualities come from an overturning of all traditionals in the name of the freedom of the individual spirit.) Gide's article

—"Dada"—encouraged the movement's supporters to refuse to be confined and to abolish every tie to the past.

Gide's support of Dadaism, his theories, and his own personal life, aided the existential trend through breaking down conventions and traditions in the myths. One effective way to break down absolutes is to give their original meanings a new twist. The French dramatists (Cocteau, Anouilh, and Giraudoux), with Gide a leader, sneered at old meanings, but gave the myths more humanity, if more profanity. In an excellent account in *The Classical Tradition,* Gilbert Highet traces the reinterpretation of the myths. Gide's *Oedipus* indicates one coming from nowhere, one with no traditions, one with no past history, one with no outside support, and therefore, one in a magnificent position. We are close to the existentialist here. In the epic and traditional sense, the hero stood with the basic essentials of his society.

Gide was as effective as Ibsen in striking at the Victorian inhibitions: in those Victorian prohibitions were supports for traditional conduct, particularly in the social life of the family. There is vitality in Gide, as opposed to the more philosophic nature of Nietzsche. Part of the violent irresponsibility of Gide came from his problem with love. The existentialist is not eager and not able to find a way to involve himself in love with someone else. The relationship must be one he can enter, but one he can leave with no possibility that he will start out as subject and end as object. Gide, religious in nature, and equally irreligious, did much to aid Sartre in abolishing God. His use of the myth was such as to take away dignity and any touch of the sacred. However, Gide's work with the myth was not as disastrous as his view of Christianity in literature. He stated, and with undeniable force, that for a Christian to be a tragic figure is nearly impossible. If a person repents with any degree of sincerity, the soul is saved. In theory, if a person can escape the temporal law, he could commit any number of serious offenses and have his soul saved if he repented.

Franz Kafka

The work of Kafka (1883–1924) is significant and puzzling, from our point of view. He has many existential qualities, but many other qualities as well. Barring him from posing as a pure existentialist is the extent of symbolism in his work. In "In the Penal Colony," one can find at least forty symbols well-authenticated as traditional. Now, symbolism is avoided by the real "true-blue" existentialist. Such is the case, as we have noted many times, because the author is forced out of himself to set up external criteria. We must modify this position long enough to indicate that symbols can be accepted when they are viewed as important for one choice or for one time only. But Kafka's position seems to be quite persistent and absolute for his works. Before looking at some of his specific works, we note that he died well before the rush and rash of the modern existentialists who appeared in full force in the post-1939 days.

Kafka was the forerunner of the surrealists. He was also deeply engaged in the world of dreams, a world where the Sartrians are not too anxious to be found. His works have anguish, dread, fear, and guilt. We find that there are strong Freudian notes in his major writings. Despite Kafka's religious nature, we discover the notes of "myth" in his writing. There are many differences between "myth" and "religion," but most dramatic of them are the features of concrete detail, specific situations, appeal to the senses, and a tragic mode of a grim individual. In myth we have more tragedy than epical qualities. Kafka's figures drive on their determined courses, in spite of suffering agony and recognition.

Love is always difficult for the existentialist as a concept. Kierkegaard did consider love the stuff of dreams, that which covers many sins; and that which is given to everyone to do and have. Finally, he expanded his statements on love: love makes man stronger or weaker than any other force. Love is that which endures through all time. Love turns darkness to light. Kafka's worlds are always dark: when love comes, death is never far away. What a man loves for someone else, he loses for himself; what a man loses as love for himself, he also loses for himself. Physical sharing is impossible with Kafka. A person sees something; he does not do that something in mutual relationships with anyone else.

As Sartre pointed out, the "other" is always trouble. For Kafka, the "other" was nearly an impossibility. Much of the darkness in Kafka's world represents his never knowing the "other." Apparently, he is never known by the "other," either. This fact is as troublesome to Kafka's heroes as is their not knowing the "other." Even when one sees transfiguration, that transfiguration is never seen in the self. Furthermore, when that insight, just before death, illuminates reality in the one individual, the observer cannot know that enlightened one.

Luigi Pirandello

Pirandello (1867–1936), a towering literary figure and dramatist, wrote plays for twenty-seven years. The Theatre of the Grotesque has its inception in Pirandello's work, where the laughter at man's oppositions becomes so inevitable because man cannot bear not to laugh. His plays indicate the contrast between reality and illusion; the sad and the humorous; the real face and its mask—and between the horror and the glory. Pirandello stays with the concrete in his plays in order to show the pain and agony of the self. He had existential qualities in his bewilderment between what is and what is not, and between his characters who strive for some identification.

His existentialism is pervasive, if sometimes indirect. When each character holds ideas as conflicting, and completes enacting his role in the play, there are no more objective ideas than there would have been passions. Children who hate their parents, husbands who aid in their own cuckolding, families which are in conflict rather than in cooperation, and criminals who prosper are in the majority. Pirandello refutes the world of accepted values, throwing the meaning of life on the individual. Since each person or concept has no meaning the same for two people, truth is a matter for the individual. To say that Pirandello asserts that a daughter must hate her mother as logically as she would love her is to be in error. To say that he is a relativist has little meaning unless we know whether this relativism is a matter between people only, or also a matter of the inner life of the same individual. His plays reach the same position that Sartre's reach, although anguish as such is not the most marked quality of his drama.

Right You Are If You Think You Are. This play reveals that objective truth as objective reality is not possible. Laudisi speaks for the heart of the thesis: there is no such thing as truth. At the conclusion of the play, what would appear to be the true solution would be to decide which is insane, the mother or the daughter. The daughter thwarts that procedure by saying that the one who is crazy is the one the "gossips" choose as insane. Thus, reality is the matter for each individual in action, as determined in social situations.

Six Characters in Search of an Author. This play finds five people interrupting a group of actors who are rehearsing for a play. The five people insist that they are characters who need an author and who need to be put in a play. The characters tell their story—and a seamy story indeed! Pirandello, hammering away at the myth of family purity and cohesiveness, develops sexual depravity on the part of the Father and Mother. Eventually, innocent children are caught up and destroyed. Emotional reconciliation is as evil as their acrimonious parting years earlier. His use of the title instead of the name depersonalizes the members as individuals and then, skillfully, destroys them as ideas. At one stroke he destroys the traditional physical, emotional, and intellectual concept of the attributes of the family. The actors then attempt to put on the play. They fail. Why do they fail? The usual criticism that the actors fail because of the conventions of the stage is not true. Such criticism overlooks a fundamental truth. Each member of the family has experienced a truth for that member, a truth that is not a part of that storehouse of moral, religious, and social principles held by a society generally and referred to by the actors specifically. Thus, the actors must fail.

Ugo Betti

Betti (1892–1913) is a universalist by implication; his plays are regional in location, centering in the isolated and rugged part of Italy where the playwright was born—Camerino. His early influences were reflected in his later vigorous and athletic life. He has strong tastes for the Teutons, particularly Nietzsche, for Sorel, and for the Italian Futurists. He was also affected by, and affected, D'Annunzio.

Betti differs from the pure existentialist in that he stresses an external grim destiny, one that is real, and one that chooses the path that man must take. Betti was far more of an existential thinker than his plays indicate. We must remember that he lived under Fascism, and too much individual standing-out was not permissible. In his *Frana allo scalo nord* he asks the question whether or not justice is possible in an absurd world. He was forced to display tremendous courage in Mussolini's regime in order to put on such a play. However, his being a judge and his having been thoroughly acquainted with all judicial administration gave him a right that others would not have had—the right of knowledge. He considers that justice is not possible, but that justice is essential. At the center of his thinking always must be that existential idea so essential to the selfhood: responsibility. A lawyer and judge spend their entire lives working around, with, and in the traditions of responsibility. In the play under discussion, a landslide kills many laborers, injures more, and renders some mentally unbalanced. The law insists on investigation, indictment, trial, and punishment of those "responsible." Goetz is the prosecutor—we note the Germanic name—and Parsc the judge.

The group stands together, but not in cowardice or in resignation. Each person and two or three people questioned in groups accuse themselves, demanding that they be found guilty. They also accuse the others; so each stands out against himself and then against all the others. The judge is baffled because the entire world must be condemned: since that is the case, a higher tribunal is essential, or a different force, pity, is required to deal with the situation. Again, we have a blend of naturalism and existentialism. In one sense we have naturalism because the assertion against natural force or the surrender to natural force is man, not individuals.

Existentially, there is the powerful speaking out in terms of the self, and a militant decision in terms of the self, even though there is also condemnation of the other. As his plays developed, his ideas became more abstract, and the situations somewhat less realistic. But, with respect to the Theatre of the Absurd, his situations are highly concrete.

Crime on Goat Island. This play has elements of naturalism, romanticism, and existentialism. Justice must take place, one way or another. Water is polyvalent: water cleanses; water destroys; water preserves; water also represents a return to the preworld state with its symbolization of death and annihilation. Then again, water must annihilate before regeneration can take place. The well, according to the anthropologist and symbolist Schneider, represents the soul and the quality of that which is feminine. Water plays a large part in many of Betti's plays, and does so in this particularly significant drama. Returning home from war, Angelo goes to the home of his dead friend. He seduces the wife, sister, and daughter of the dead soldier. Finally, he meets his fate and retribution in the family well.

Because of the world in which we live, and because of the mind that we have, man finds difficulty in resolving what he will do and what he ought to do. What he will do and what he ought to do, do not often coincide: but after he does what he ought not to do, there must be justice. The world, then, is irrational; all is absurd, and the individual is held to account for not being able to stand—in time—ahead of his decision, so that he will avoid retribution. Thus, all responsibility eventually devolves on the individual, and does so because only an individual is rewarded or punished. Betti's rugged individualism leads him to the brink of the existential process of living, but stops short of divorcing the individual from outside binding criteria.

For Sartre and Genet, the individual is his law, and the individual "exists" the law. But, for Betti, the law stands outside and works to the inside of the individual.

François Mauriac

Mauriac (1885–   ) was born in France. He is a Christian and Catholic writer, one of the few significant in France. As such, he has faced French anticlericalism, Catholic criticism, and the analysis of his own works for both religious and literary value. As with T. S. Eliot, he has considered the modern wasteland, a wasteland in the throes of spiritual aridity and spiritual deprivation. Whereas Eliot took a greater geographical area for his wasteland, Mauriac has confined his desert to his own region of France. He has a Miltonian hatred of that which is sensual, but an irresistible attraction toward such sensuality. The poetic spirit in him gives him a more dramatic and universal tenor than is ordinarily present in purely prose works. Mauriac is able to show more despair, distress, and more sin through appealing, at the same time, to spirit, body, and mind.

The main criticisms often levied against Mauriac and his art are that he makes vice attractive: this criticism is a severe one from the point of view of the Church, and from an artistic point of view as well. The objection is not to the content of life, but to the tone of its presentation. As a Catholic born, Mauriac, state the critics, should not be engrossed with sin in a heretical way; he presents what he should not know, whereas Greene and Waugh can present the stuff of life they know because of their experiences as Catholic and Protestant. We shall look to Mauriac's specific qualities.

His existentialism is evident in his preference for himself; at this position he has great difficulty with Christian critics, because, assertedly a Christian, Mauriac votes for self in such a way as to indicate that religion can live through the vote of the individual only.

Mauriac reflects the view that one cannot love Christ until he loves himself. Not until he senses his worth can he assess himself as worthy of eternity. Indirectly, he refutes Leigh Hunt's position ("Abou Ben Adhem") that love of man is not enough. Love of self is a prerequisite to God and Christ.

Mauriac has the faculty of seeing conflict in every experience: the entire consciousness is torment, tension, and battle. In order to render the conflict dramatically sensational, Mauriac, like the existential, generally, insists on the physical sensation in sex, opposed by opposition.

Mauriac, like Blake, Rousseau, and Greene, was extremely sensitive to childhood. His works reflect the idea that the child does come trailing clouds of glory and innocence. However, the innocence is lost before such innocence is understood. We have the brooding sense of isolation and alienation: first, from innocence and then from childhood.

Mauriac recommended publicly, and in his works, that modern man is greater than his forebears because he has a penchant for agonizing. In order to agonize with greater intensity, he will shut out knowledge of any factor that will alleviate the suffering; rejecting social forces for his guide, Mauriac insisted that since life is despair and anguish, we might very well provide our own.

For the most part, Mauriac is satisfied with the conflicts and tensions with the individual and among individuals. He believes that whatever salvation can be achieved is rooted within the sexual desires themselves. He does not usually allow his characters to consume each other since to do so would take the attention away from the conflict, and would further make redemption possible. *The River of Fire* is the only work where the heroine is completely given over to unrestrained passion. Then she recoils, and withdraws completely from life. She is apparently saved by the very fire she has gone through. The inner vision and the self assertion that pays tribute to her free will, will win through to salvation.

Despair, anguish, repentance, and remorse result from love affairs in all Mauriac's novels. The affairs are more the results of fires of imaginative passion than real physical encounters. In the Judaic-Christian tradition we have seen that guilt can be mental and emotional. For the Greek, the act must take place for guilt. Not until Antigone buried her brother did she know that she "was dead." When the fires of internal conflict have burnt out, all is dead. The internal conflict is a prerequisite to spiritual communion. One must sin before he can be saved. The destruction of the body appears to be that which is needed.

Chapter 6

■

Modern Literary Existentialism in Continental Europe

France

ANDRÉ MALRAUX

Malraux's wide travels, his adventurous nature, and his opposition to Fascism and Nazism stand behind the material for his literary output. His writings have been biased toward Marxism, but his later works show a turn away from Communism. Malraux finds man set in such a framework of historicity that violence through wars, natural disasters, ideological conflicts and death are his everyday companions. However, Malraux outdid his historicity somewhat, for his heroes travel everywhere to commit themselves to action, to seek out conflict. Only through tossing the self and body into the arena of killing, living, dying, suffering, and agonizing can a man derive some real meaning from life and give meaning to life.

The only way that man can win to a sense of himself that he can tolerate is to assert his own death as one of value. When he asserts his death, he is no longer bound, but free, because he wills to bespeak his own destiny.

Malraux differs from other existentialists we have considered in detail: first, because of his strong anti-Nazism and Fascism; second, because he concerns himself intimately with class structures as such. While other modern writers will commit themselves to philosophical and sociological concerns, Malraux evaluates his characters against their conduct in the radical movements to which they attach themselves. There is the individual; there is his group; then there is the other group—and the other individual. His characters do not exist apart from their class identification.

Malraux's position is that he will take the world solely on a horizontal level. He will remove all absolutes as institutions, except the political and social class. He then insists that if a_1, a_2, a_3, and so on . . . individuals make up a class, that the class has more value than all the individuals added together within the set. When one is heroic for the group, he is heroic for all. The heroism has been committed to the group and is a part of its structure. Such a position is unique. Whatever is done in the name of the group, whether understood by its members or not, is a matter of significance. Even if defeated on the tactical field, they win because they have faced the fact of death, and have themselves chosen their own deaths.

Malraux believes that in any activity, war or art, struggle is the ingredient needed in creativity. To revolt in art means a breaking down, a revolt, a revolution, and a sad isolation. His theory is that the themes should be of low and suffering humanity. Why? When the great figures finally disappear, who is left? The painter remains: thus the task of the artist is not the painting of objects, but "painting." The painter is a creator; thus, he should not allow his painting of objects to possess him. The artist's task is not to be trapped into his own products, but to remain supreme as creating, possessing, and "existing" the painting. One can be devoured *in* his painting, but he must not be devoured *by* his painting. The artist's novels work in the same fashion.

Malraux, international in spirit, is essentially human in his art. Hurling himself into fundamental questions, this novelist proceeds to settle the problems with men in action. His poetry enables him to reach the universal point, and, at the same time, gives imaginative luster to the fact, to the concrete detail.

Without his poetry, Malraux's humanity would not be enough because the group thesis would overpower the humanity of the single individual. However, because of his poetic and artistic nature, Malraux is able to define the individual so that he exists as uniquely human and significant. How do the dead have meaning? How are they preserved? Death has a past when living in the memory of "Awareness of Being-ness." Death changes the life into some value called Destiny. This Destiny lives, rests, and depends upon the hands of the living. How can this position exist? Here we find the group or the class valuable. The reason that the group is more than the sum of its living members comes from meaning and value of Death. In fact, Malraux looks at Death as being human, that which is a structure of the individual life, that which, when active, changes life to the Destiny we have noted.

In noting his qualities, we find that Malraux is an existentialist. We would believe that such a state would be difficult for a view that insists on group or class structure. But the group is composed of more than individuals, the "more" being the meaning that individuals have given to the structure. Although there are specific issues involved, such as economic, political, and social problems, the real battle is against life itself. Man must die, and he has his living bounds circumscribed, often in such a way that his only meaning is protesting. He cannot win in the individual life, but assessing its historical reason for being, man battles against all the "isms." The battling is more significant than the specific results—which are usually fatal for the individuals in his stories.

ALBERT CAMUS

Camus (1913–1960) was a French-Algerian novelist, critic, dramatist, and essayist; he was unquestionably the greatest modern French writer, with the possible exception of Sartre.

Camus believes that we can exist "authentically" only if we stand up and out to life by agreeing that suicide is a possibility of man, that all life is absurd, that the world is totally absurd, and that we should, individually, persist in being human in spite of these formidable obstacles. Our very "seeking for" indicates that despite the meaninglessness of life, such meaning as there is must be that of the human being who experiences the absurdity. He believes that we can find truth and justification for existence and existing if we do not insist on having absolutes that demand working toward clearly defined ends. In fact, driving one's self to obtain ends set up outside of the self by other agencies is the major part of being absurd. Camus, like all French writers, has his view of art. Camus reveals the world as absurd, but does leave man as human, thus countering naturalism which shows man as entirely depersonalized. To the usual existential themes of violence and death, the extra ingredient added by Camus is that of absurdity. In method we find him stressing immediacy of experience and the reliance on the concrete detail and fact; some physical, others the facts of consciousness.

Camus believes, in his works, that the following criteria are valid:

1. God does not exist or his existence is not significant.

2. The absolutes, such as the Ten Commandments and other church dogma, are dead.

3. The universe, now that the deity is destroyed or has abdicated, must be brought to order.

4. Man, as a human being, and as a unique animal that is human, has utter responsibility. He has no outside ethical, metaphysical, supernatural, or prophet-like aids. He must save himself with only himself for company.

5. What Malraux termed Destiny is akin to what Camus calls the duty to establish some order in each individual, absurd, chaotic life.

6. As we noted in our brief opening survey, Camus views the world as absurd because man must always roll up a force which rolls back down on him—reality. Sisyphus had to roll the stone up the hill, perpetually, to no physical avail.

7. Although this punishment to which each man is condemned is absurd, through such negatory actions man can affirm himself as a choosing and responsible self by facing up to his dilemma.

Camus followed the French course of trying to resolve the split in human personality. He goes back to time immemorial in trying to decide what emphasis should be given the intellect and the dynamic part of man. Camus started with the extremes, a position always somewhat untenable. He sought to find a middle position. Here we have the French rational approach which is usually pushed to its extreme—irrationalism. Camus insisted that man is totally at war with himself. He loves life intensely, and he abhors life: thus the starting point is bitter conflict.

SIMONE DE BEAUVOIR

De Beauvoir (1908–   ) is a French essayist, novelist, and dramatist. She is unquestionably the existentialist per se. Man is tossed into the absurd world, and the toss costs him the death of the self. Whatever objectives toward which he drives, each man must create them. In creating his own goals, he exists himself, but his despair comes because he can not step ahead at six o'clock and know the results of his choices when he is only at five o'clock.

In *The Second Sex,* the novelist reveals, frankly, woman from three points of view: the biological, the psycho-analytical, and the materialistic-historical. Woman is always made the "Other" by man, so that she can be made object, devoured, and possessed. Her position results from the action of man, who, in making her "Other," induces her to enter a second-rate position. She is, from the very beginning, alienated twice: naturally, in an absurd world; and by force, through the ways of man. The novelist is trying to purge our culture of the old myth of Adam and Eve wherein Eve received all the blame for inducing evil, disobedience, wilfullness, and sensuality. She also insists that we remove all mythological figures who have been made inferior, as woman, to man.

JEAN GIRAUDOUX

Teacher, essayist, novelist, and playwright, this brilliant Frenchman, Giraudoux (1882–1944), enriched his many environments. A true Renaissance spirit, his qualities included spontaneous irony, allusion, paradox, a rich mythological background. His works include historical backgrounds, Biblical backgrounds, and some material deliberately thrown out of time context to obtain universal significance. Aiding him in obtaining universal truth are his techniques of altering the myth, appealing to the tragic sense of the individual, heightening emotional responses through poetry, and avoiding local topics as such. His books and plays reflect a nature fundamentally philosophical.

The element of conflict is usually carried within Giraudoux's hero; the universe suffers because he does, and the heroes have tragic destiny with them. Each considers that he is involved in being all things at the same time, but the things are opposite. Whereas in some writers, theories, and countries, there is a time to live and a time to die, this author's heroes try to live with both at once. Man contends with Satan and God; with man and the metaphysical; with calm and storm; with love and hate; with peace and war. Giraudoux was an intellectual. He takes the myths and modifies the basic material to show not what was accomplished but what could have been accomplished. Giraudoux handles Judith in much the same way as Browning handled the girl in "Porphyria's Lover." Each is slain to preserve the memory of a night of love.

JEAN ANOUILH

Anouilh (1910–   ) was influenced by Giraudoux to write plays. He has the French emphasis on opposites even more dramatically represented than by Giraudoux. Anouilh uses symbolism more than does Giraudoux. One of the features of his symbolism is embodied in his contrast of good and evil, reward and punishment, the pure individual and the protesting society. The red pieces stand for that which is good; the black for that which is evil; again, no compromise is possible. Anouilh "rehabilitates" old myths.

Does Anouilh hurl his genius at an effort to move man to the absolute? Or does he lower his aim and make a good "social playwright"? One way or another, we are moved to ask this question of all modern French playwrights. We find out that for Anouilh there are many sins and many sinners: generally, they receive the traditional payment and wages—death. For characters this playwright does not comb the temples, the houses of nobility, the halls of the universities for his material; frequently they are of good peasant stock, good yeoman stock, bad peasant stock, and bad yeoman stock. They do have one marked quality. They are willing to lower their heads and hearts and drive hard at life. They swerve neither to the right nor to the left, but throw their all into a savage collision.

JEAN PAUL SARTRE (1905–   )

Sartre starts from the thesis that we cannot see our predicament from the outside. That we can transcend seeking and being by gaining freedom by action has no logic in itself; but action enables each man to be aware of himself, and being aware is more significant than being aware of something. Significance always comes about by gaining an immediacy of consciousness through actions which, for the most part, are seamy. When a man cannot commit himself to and through action and acting, his is a world of nausea (a title, incidentally, of one of Sartre's novels). Sartre is not interested one way or another in actions as good or as bad, but only as making the individual conscious of existence, even if only conscious of an absurd existence. If the actions requiring such consciousness are evil, then the individual must involve himself in evilness since gaining immediacy of experience is more important than absolutes such as good or evil. Therefore, we can understand why Sartre accepts Genet.

Sartre indicates that we have accepted Genet as an artist, but not as a depraved rogue. Sartre's sparkling but wicked humor takes over. Not only has Genet not been accepted as evil because the reader had done the re-creation himself, but the really good people have never accepted him in any way because they can not and do not read. Thus he is not avenged on the part of society. Having eliminated good and evil, poor Genet can no longer sin. Finally, he fails because society, through the efforts of Sartre and other artists, has had Genet given a pardon; thus, he is possessed by the charity and mercy of the state. If there was no god, history shows, that man would create one. Man is totally unable to live without the concepts of sin and evil. That is one reason why he is absurd. Thus, who can say that Sartre is absurd when he insists that we keep the Ten Commandments and other laws around so that he will have something to stand out against? One sad observation is that whatever Sartre does or does not prove, he makes out a critical case. Real experiences furnish, as C. S. Lewis would say, "grounds for the human imagination." Experiences are always found in two categories: those that are good, and those that are evil. Sartre believes that there is enough of the corrupt in man that he is quite happy to use his creative faculties in search of horror instead of glory. He is willing to pursue damnation instead of salvation.

JEAN GENET

Push a philosophy far enough and the philosophy becomes its opposite; push Genet's evil far enough, and we are in the presence of that which is good. Going far beyond the French Symbolists, surpassing Wilde, and making art itself equal with evil, Genet (1909–   ) has found himself in the awkward position of creating a nullity in his own terms. He has often stated that when everything is bad, nothing is bad. If he creates a world of entire evil, we demand the opposite. He can be conscious of himself as an identity by insisting that were all speculations of any kind to disappear as reality he would be conscious, at least, of his ability to doubt. Being conscious of his doubting, he would be conscious of his own thinking. Finally, being conscious of his own thinking, he would be conscious of his existence, as real. Genet uses somewhat the same line of reasoning for his identity. Genet insists that when all values are negated, he can sin; therefore he is. Genet turns into art what came to him as a heritage from Ibsen, Strindberg, Sade, Baudelaire, Camus, Gide, and the other French writers, as well as Nietzsche and Dostoevsky. When there is complete evil, there is all that goes to make up evil: sadism, masochism, perversion, assault, larceny, robbery, hypocrisy—all the negatives of life. Not to include them all would be an artistic offense. Genet realizes that society stands against him, as did Anouilh. We have seen that society is a corrupt institution. If society is a corrupt institution, and if Genet stands against society, what is he? If he is not a sinner, then he is a saint. Here we have a challenge as to point of view. If society's offense-taking is on a grand scale, then the inherent capacity for evil in society is on a grand scale. Thus Genet does not create evil, but does create the grounds for the reader's evil imagination, or offers a challenge to the reader to recreate on his own evil terms. Genet is often accused of glorying in the triumph of evil; but that is not the same as being evil, or of creating evil. For the artist, all the materials of experience are available; if some of them are irrational enough and absurd enough to be evil, then evil is furnished not as utilitarian, but as art.

If Genet were a saint, which he is not, he could insist that all his characters who are cast out from society must be saints; and the society, the sinner. In trying to make society accept evil, he offers society the chance to compromise itself. Society has accepted a view of itself from many angry writers over all human history. Its love for money, for power, and for hypocrisy have characterized its total structure and all of its classes. If all of its dicta are set aside and a new world of evil commenced, then is the objection merely one of degree and not of substance? If the amount of evil is 100 per cent rather than 90 per cent what is objected to?

Consider the matter of evil. Either Genet is holding up a mirror of total evil, the ultimate in depravity, to society, or he is holding up a society which is evil by definition only of society. Or he is holding up that which is good. If to know one's self is good, then the face of evil should be good. Of course, we cannot let Genet get away that easily. Genet was a criminal, a confirmed criminal and a somewhat exultant one. He was also an artist, a poet. From a point of view of personal history, Genet fulfilled all the qualifications of not only standing outside of society, but of "being stood" outside. He was born illegitimate, brought up by ordinary workers, sent to prison for stealing when he was nine or ten years of age, and, from then on, he was an inmate of many jails over a widespread area. He wrote *Our Lady of the Flowers* in jail. He was sentenced to life imprisonment as a habitual criminal. Finally, many of France's greatest writers secured his release.

Genet's characters desire murder, but they also want to be murdered. This pathological devouring and being devoured is in reality a desperate desire for individuality, an assertion of human freedom. If he will be destroyed, he as subject will make the choice. Genet's predicament is his inability to pacify opposite claims. Genet wants to have a complete metamorphosis of all values, including all values found in dogmas, creeds, and institutions. But what is he going to change? He is going to change an absolute order, one Sartre will not admit as existing. He must face the absolute and permanent order of law, policemen, store detectives, social classes, and jails, as well as clergymen and churches. He cannot change what is changing. To change something, there must be a solid "that-ness" to change. Thus, he must have—and must even insist upon—an order backed by law and morality. In order to destroy, there must be something to destroy. If he desires primitivism, unlimited sensuality, and unrestrained violence, he must have the opposition always out there facing him. Genet's plays idolize blasphemy, profanity, and sacrilege, but he must retain that which can be blasphemed against, sworn against, and made the object of sacrilege. Thus Genet faces a world of faith, belief and opinion.

ARTHUR ADAMOV

Adamov (1908–   ), born of Armenian parents, was brought up in French culture, after receiving some education in Switzerland and Germany. He belonged to the 1920's Surrealist movement, wrote poetry, and headed an avante-garde drama periodical. *The Confession* is an honest and terrifying revelation of a spiritual autobiography. He declared his alienation, his inability to find an identity, the piling up of time as unactualized, and the failure of language to express himself. Language did not reach him. We meet the familiar desire to be humiliated by the lowest forms of life, to be possessed and not to possess. Man has been isolated from the rich and ambiguous myths and legends of the past. He now has no spiritual roots.

Society and the human predicament have man gripped in a vise; he knows not which way to turn. Man is forced to live in a society where language is not adequate to handle a nature red in tooth and claw, vicious from its very nature. Family love is itself a strangling influence. Man must not seek the facile way out. He must look at the total personality: mind, heart, and hand. He must also consider the psychic, the religious, the economic, and the social animal that man is. He must consider man and his supernatural; man and his fellow man; and man and the inner soul. But we have nothing but a world of appearances here. We must break open these chimeras, tear the veils apart to see the form behind.

The world is absurd, but Adamov will not go all the way, for to have no meaning means total annihilation. He is a capable enough political thinker to vote for an ideology, so he chooses Communism. He is too much of an individualist to commit himself to such an externality; thus, his is a subjective preference.

Adamov uses a world of dreams, but buttresses them with reality, much more so than does Genet. We have the old in new arrangements; the common takes an uncommon turn because the world of ordinary experience is seen as highly irrational. A recurrent theme is that of the alienation caused when a person finds, consciously, that what he has as an image of himself is not that which others have. Seeking communication to support a reasonable psychic view of himself, he discovers that society and institutions give him a mirror in which he appears as a blank. Character has little to do with the crucial question of identity because the extrovert and the introvert came to the same useless frustrations. The individual who is caught between warring groups takes on their suffering without his consent.

JEAN TARDIEU

Tardieu (1903–   ), poet and dramatist, is also in the tradition of the Theatre of the Absurd. His main contribution comes in the realm of the one-act play and in his effort to modify the realistic theatre to the new forms in human experience, and to the most effective ways for their expression. Tardieu believes that the one-act play is most effective when presenting a situation or a problem, working from the inside out; by the end of the presentation, several larger issues are usually implied. He also has a philosophy, one not far removed from that of his contemporaries. First, rationality is difficult in a world dominated by irrational ideologies and their violent pressures. There is no hope for man in a world that is without reason and meaning. Tardieu is more positive than the other writers, perhaps because he is a genuine poet. Man finds himself in a universe that is a floating and formless mass of hostility; man can save himself by love—if he will forego the macrocosmic world.

Qui est la? (Who Is There?) presents man in an engulfing void. We have father, mother, and child, quite ordinary and entirely depersonalized without names. The family, in bare surroundings, is at the table. While they are munching their pieces of bread and eating the rest of a modest meal, a woman dashes in and warns the three. A paid assassin strangles the father on the spot. He is thrown out on the earth, with many other corpses; they are not buried. While the mother and son look out, the father, without life, jumps up and informs the audience that although man is dead, someday he will again "be." The mother and son ask him for information: who killed him and who is he, the speaker? We are reminded of the situation in *The Wasteland*. When the right question is asked, there will be means whereby we can establish ourselves with the values that once meant something.

Roumania

EUGENE IONESCO

Ionesco (1912–   ) was born in Roumania. If, as he suggests, his works are not explicit, and if, as the readers and audiences discover, his work is entirely ambiguous, so is man. Ionesco is interested in a whole man, not one merely tossed into society and one trapped as a social thing. Because he takes a macroscopic view of man and his possibilities, Ionesco's work is the more pessimistic. When any malign force or event wounds an institution, thing, person, or idea, each individual dies a bit. Man is in a terrible predicament. He is not so much in despair, because there is a gulf between what he wants and what he can obtain, as he is in alienation from a world that can offer no permanent solution to any one desire and no solution to man's total complex of desires. As we have seen before, in the existential mind, man is a born loser. If a writer attacks Communism, democracy, the Klan, the NAACP, democracy, socialism, or some specific ideology or "ism," his point of view can be evaluated. If, as in Ionesco's plays, all externality is attacked, then society is totally condemned, and the entire world of reality is a sinking phenomenon.

Ionesco is one of the few dramatists to rationalize his own writing critically. His position is that the critic should be content to explain what has been done by the dramatist, not to indicate what "should" or "ought" to be done, except with the premises inherent in the play. If he believes that the world is empty, meaningless, and like a collapsible drinking cup, then he has to look to all points at once; and thus to no points, because the blind forces externally are equated by blind forces tearing up his inner consciousness. We do not know whether the world is torn and sinking because of his own consciousness, which projects such a world, or whether he is convinced that the absurdity of the world is that which reacts on or against the individual.

When he looks for substantiality, none exists; he is up against nothingness—as one condemned to throw a tennis ball in the air continually; finally, nothing is evident except pain. When man seeks isolation or nothingness, the weight of reality bears upon him. There are Freudian notes, echoes of Strindberg, and parent and child images, particularly the mother-image or figure. In some instances that which is of no importance is mushroomed into eternity; in other cases, the potentially important dwindles, excruciatingly, into nothing at all—the potentials merely drop off the human horizon.

In spoken and written defense of his position, Ionesco has made, substantially, the following points:

1. He does not deliberately oppose realism; quite the contrary.

2. Communication by language is not impossible, but only difficult for the whole man in such a world.

3. Man is larger than the world of society to which and through which critics believe that man should operate and express himself.

4. Because man makes society, and not man, a better society will have to demand a better language. The language will need to differ from that which traditionally has brought man to his present impasse.

5. When man destroys dead sayings, stereotypes, and empty adages, he finds the great truth of the archetype. He kills the stereotype to get to the universal.

6. Society's language is absurd, serving to alienate man from himself—to dwarf his world. Absurd language, as such, at

its very least, forces the audience to consider its own condition. The absurdity of his language, Ionesco's, is nowhere nearly as ridiculous as the dead skin of language man grows within.

7. Expressionism is part of Ionesco's art, but an expressionism that is quite abstract.

8. Altogether, Ionesco's art leaves no person an opportunity to become wound up in and with any particular thesis. He opposes the revealing and discussing of theories, ideologies, and dogma through making the language in each ridiculous, and through making those who discuss life in past terms as ridiculous as the terms he uses.

Ionesco was born of a French mother and Roumanian father. Much of his early life was spent in France. A sensitive person from the very first, he was always seized with anxiety and a love for mummery and theatre. The contrast between his intellectual world and the brutal peasant world was dramatic and traumatic. He attended school in both France and Roumania, and finally attended the University in Bucharest.

When we consider some of his earlier experiences, we are able to understand the direction his art was to take. He delighted in presenting opposite sides. First he would attack the local poets and dramatists of his time; then, a short time later, he would laud and eulogize them. He discussed, with some effect, how to hold different views, at the same time, on political, social, economic, and religious events. He started early in making himself a battleground—two men within. We have Ionesco reducing himself to nullity through the conflicts of equally strong but opposing views. Small wonder that he has always felt torn from within.

He became a teacher and, having returned to France, he found himself in the publishing industry through World War II. He had not turned his hand to writing, certainly not to drama. Trying to learn English, he started to write a play. There are two characters, wife and husband, the Smiths. There are also statements about children, servant, friends, and about the ordinary details of English life. Lo! The playwright learns that mankind everywhere is engaged in the same, ordinary, and meaningless conversations and actions. The same old phrases were there, but in a different tongue. All rational meaning collapsed as language broke up into as many isolated bits as does man's self-consciousness. The entire structural fragmentation on language equated the sinking of the world into nothingness, much as one feels in being forced to stand still while water rises from the floor, up and up, until man is submerged.

Germany

MAX FRISCH

In the modern theatre, there are two significant German names: Max Frisch and Friedrich Durrenmatt; their modest number of works belongs in the Theatre of the Absurd. Frisch (1911—) is both German and Swiss, but finds his popularity in the German theatrical world. The Swiss are too practical and empirical for his drama of anguish, distress, and despair. Frisch commits himself entirely to his plays, and his plays take on a passionate subjectivity that sometimes flaws his work. His works provide pity and horror, and stress that man's position today is such that he cannot make an intelligent deduction from the world in which he lives. He does not know what he should do or should not do. No matter how much he encounters experience, he is no wiser than he was before. Thus, he must despair: at the most, the correct decision would, for him, merely be a fortuitous one. Man is totally inadequate to justify standing out—even if he could, which he cannot do.

Frisch's position is not difficult; we have met the conditions several times before. Reduced to its simplest terms, his position is that man is frustrated because he cannot do what he wants to do, and he has to do what he does not want to do. He cannot be where he wants to be, and he must be where he does not want to be. He desires to shut himself up in himself, and he is not free with himself. Money, marriage, and manners, or comedy across the board, are all considered in Frisch's plays. He wants the pleasure of sex without the responsibilities, a position by no means unique.

FRIEDRICH DURRENMATT

Death is at the center of the plays and thoughts of Durrenmatt (1921—) and, steeped in the knowledge of pan-Teutonism, he knows that power "doth corrupt utterly," particularly when that power is absolute. What we should note is that the position seems nearly hopeless in the light of the views he holds *ab initio*. If death is a creeping influence, resulting only in the final act, there is no reason why power, if desired, should not be absolute. If death is a condition that makes every human situation, experience, and reaction of little significance, man still need not abandon power. Man may be conscious of life's grim limitations. He may feel conscious of the slowly-descending shades of annihilation. Can he still use his powerful will to oppose the odds that death sets against him? Yes, he can still use his power and will in one of two ways: he may make his own choice on his own terms to surrender completely, or he may hurl himself in reckless and contemptuous daring against death itself.

Spain

MANUEL DE PEDROLO

Because of an inherent conservatism in the Spanish temperament, because of an establishmentarianism in Church and State, Spanish literature has not taken on the cynical and skeptical doubts inherent in French intellectualism. With the Spanish Civil War won by France, the Church has maintained power, but a weakened power. The playwrights, few in number, have been freer to the horizontal world, or freer to decry the inadequacies of the vertical world, or the supernatural. We shall consider, briefly, De Pedrolo and Arrabal, then move on to Lorca.

De Pedrolo (1918—) novelist, short-story writer, and playwright has both a Renaissance spirit and the varied career of the sixteenth-century adventurer. He battled for the Loyalists, to no avail. He has sold insurance, patent medicine, stocks, weapons, and shoelaces. On the more intellectual level he has read for publishing houses, and he has translated. His relative obscurity is the result of his writing in Catalan, a language not easy to translate, nor to understand when translated. A few of his plays have notes of the Theatre of the Absurd, for example, *Humans and No* and *Cruma*. Spanish literature, when not moral and didactic, tends to be either picaresque or naturalistic. Novels and plays stated with naturalism tend to have elements of the picaresque, in the entirely unheroic role. Little current Spanish writing is existential, but *Humans* and *No* has much of the absurd.

The Spanish tendency to visit the metaphysical, one way or another, is also present in the play. The question of freedom is involved. We would expect such a problem to be present because despite a certain determinism and fatalism in the complex Spanish character, the Spaniard tends to be individualistic, and to desire to die his own death.

The acceptance of the fact that life imposes, one after another, barriers for man to endure or to break through highlights the play *Humans and No*. A subhuman jailor, called No, tries to keep the inmates behind their bars. The jailor is in a middle section, with two sets of prisoners, one to his left and one to his right. In the first set are Fabi and Selena, and in the second set are Bret and Eliana. On their first effort to escape, they are overpowered by the alert if primitive No. Having smelled the possibility of success, each couple has future efforts in mind.

The imaginative quality of De Pedrolo asserts itself in the conclusion of the play. The two, believing they have found an avenue of escape not previously explored, tear down what they believe to be a flimsy curtain. They are shocked to find that No was correct when he told them not to pull down the curtain. For No is also a prisoner. Insight comes to the girl, Sorne. No had told her that worse than death itself would be what she would find were the curtain to be pulled. Whether we are human, or, like No, less than human, knowledge reveals that none that live can ever attain freedom. A little knowledge is a dangerous thing, even for No. Even to know that nature of a creature as primitive as No is to reveal to the Humans that that recognition of the condition called "life" is worse than death itself. What the bars represent beyond the jailing of these people is rich with ambiguity. They can represent personal suffering, intellectual suffering, or supernatural suffering, perhaps each, because there are physical, intellectual, and spiritual barriers in life. The dominant note is that of the dangers of intellectual curiosity, the barriers revealed by eating of the tree of knowledge. The subhuman No does not understand too much, but the knowledge that he has received as to what is beyond the curtain has served to shatter his faith, and to induce a hopeless pessimism.

De Pedrolo's *Cruma* is in tune with *Humans and No*—solitude, alienation, man-in-sickness, sickness from isolation. He does not know—and does not know that he does not know; his is a perceptual world that never gets beyond the things he has at hand.

FERNANDO ARRABAL

The only other Spaniard who has genuine claim to the "absurd" frame of mind is Arrabal (1932—). Having lived in France for much of his life, Arrabal has acquired a certain French intellectualism. He believes that the human predicament is hard to assess because man carries over a childish naïveté that results in a thorough assimilation of moral or ethical strictures and laws. Arrabal, unlike Blake, does not see the young child as pure and innocent, but as cruel. Arrabal is one of the few to fix on the element of cruelty in the Spanish nature, reducing that element to one inherent in the child, but brought along with maturity.

The Automobile Graveyard reverts to the question of goodness brought up in *Oraison*. Our familiarity with the many acres of wrecked and ancient cars gives the spectator or listener the impact of first-hand reality.

The absurdity is in trying to be "good." In fact, no one today understands what "goodness" means. We can interpret the play in one respect as hearkening back to the child's inherent cruelty and violence as being opposed to good. But we have a problem in such a position: in Arrabal's art, the child does not know. Knowledge is usually a prerequisite for goodness and evil. Emanou makes goodness purely "feeling." Here we have the position of a child who beams with pleasure when his world comes at his call. Goodness is made synonymous with pleasure, a simple pleasure of well-being.

Belgium

MICHEL DE GHELERODE

De Ghelerode (1898–1962) has been placed in the Theatre of the Absurd, in The New Theatre of Europe, and in The Theatre of the Grotesque. Our concern is with existential qualities; each of these theatres has plays with existential qualities. Ghelerode has all of the qualities we have mentioned as germane to the existential mind: search for self, lost identity, commitment, the question of choosing, pain, disgust of the intellect, absurdity, and lack of meaning. What keeps this playwright from being an existentialist? He believes that man is capable of a rich human relationship within the limits of a world that makes destiny as such absurd. Like Faulkner, he is not a graceful writer: he favors distortion, sadism, degenerated characters, and the rotten smell of death. He is provincial or regional in the way that Faulkner is regional; however, as with Faulkner, Ghelerode uses his narrower world to speak to the universal condition of man. His "heroes" take on the universal impact of the epic hero in the religious or morality plays. But Ghelerode's epic heroes are not "tall" but stunted and dwarfed, like Faulkner's. This playwright, as would be expected in—and with—drama, aims for exaggeration; he uses the technique of Ben Jonson and Molière, in that he stresses a particular quality of the individual. However, whereas Jonson used the character trait expressed as an abstraction, Ghelerode uses the physical trait for distortion. He has dwarfs, hunchbacks, fat people, scarecrows, individuals with skin disease and other organic and functional unpleasant appearances. Ghelerode has a heavy hand; his work does not have the deft and subtle touch of the French playwright. In his works, sensuality is even more shocking than in the hands of an Anouilh. His death is very deathly indeed. His ponderousness is always oppressive. Using the existential quality of opposition, his works reflect the ribald, but they do so with such heaviness as to make the entire effect grotesque. Profanity, sensuality, distortion, and meaninglessness are his stocks in trade as he slants the action against the Catholic Church. We shall indicate his major theses:

1. Satan is second in command in the universe, and first on earth.

2. If one man follows another, he shall come to grief, for every man is hard put to lead himself.

3. Man is the only animal whose nature is so corrupt as to isolate him from his best interests.

4. Death calls for innocence, not guilt: the guilty live on in punishing themselves.

5. Man has the capacity for divinity but is socially and morally as scab-infested as any leper.

6. His work is vulgar with its details of evacuation and urination because man prefers to be vulgar rather than refined; to be profane rather than sacred.

7. Ghelerode's satire becomes invective because he does not leave much room for man to reform himself—all of his people are fools. There is no one to laugh at others; the laughter is always at the wrong thing or at the wrong point.

8. Satan's work is so complete that each man considers himself a god, but we see the god as perverted.

9. Man substitutes drunkenness and the delirium of sexuality to increase his idea of his divinity and to supply the meaning he can not find.

10. The sardonic is revealed in unusual form: each individual joins with others in mass confessions of failings and sins.

11. Only through death has one any opportunity to shake himself loose from an evil nature.

12. Religion often acts in such a way as to prevent its avowed role—combatting Satan.

13. Beneath and behind all jest is a pervasive cruelty and sadism.

14. Beneath a persistent pessimism is a religious nature that indicates a deep love for humanity, one which is strongest when Ghelerode's views are gloomiest.

To say that Ghelerode has had troubles with the truth is no exaggeration. However, there are good priests and bad priests, and mixtures, but the good priests need no dramatizing. Goodness is a powerful entity or quality that speaks for itself and needs little advocating, merely actualizing. Ghelerode, grounded in the more provincial aspects of religion by virtue of his close association with the soil of Flanders, realized that the Church, as universal, is of fine moral timber; that its highest spokesmen are able to interpret religion to the present state of the world. However, the provincial mind remains that way, and the day-by-day work in the vineyards of saving souls is done by the unenlightened priests and their assistants. Such was his point of view, one not calculated to gain universal acceptance.

The influence of the English and Italian Renaissance is evident in Ghelerode's often made statements that the drama of the world should pull together experience, not analyze life. He believed that drama should take care of the world of dreams, but should not sort life out into nice dreams and bad dreams.

The entire range of life should be indicated. So, like T. S. Eliot, Ghelerode's range includes the glory and the horror. Although he is not much of a psychologist or a sociologist, one of his personal aversions is the impact of man's alienation and isolation when in crowds. The shock made him physically ill— a psychic nausea.

Even in his native Flanders, Ghelerode's inspiration produced the saturnine view that man's long tradition did not necessarily make for the evolution of a better man. He also believed that we can love our fellow man in more than one way. We can love him as ideal, from an intellectual and personal distance. We can love him in the intimate personal experiences at play, work, religion, and physical love. We see in Ghelerode a Swift who loves the personal individual, who struggles in working out his daily salvation, but who has a dour and a sour view of man in the abstract. Ghelerode preferred to love man at a considerable distance, the aesthetic distance of the theatre. In the majority of his plays, as in *Pantagleize,* we see a universal man in an ironic situation. He is foolish enough to find that life is pleasant. He selects May Day, today a symbol of revolt and demonstrations, for his day of disseminating his personal euphoria—all is well with the world. By the end of the day, he finds himself still believing that we have a beautiful world and that a pure heart and an innocent state make for joy in nature and joy in self. He does not think as complex people would think. But Hell and Satan take him with all the others who are slaughtered that day. Even as he is being massacred, he asserts the beauty of the day. He is correct, and that is the grotesque part. The day is lovely, but man is not.

In each of Ghelerode's characteristic works, as in *Pantagleize,* there is one of two situations existing: either the main figures are aware of the vast corruption of the sophisticated world, or they are not of the temperament to be aware of evil. For an innocent man to concern himself with destiny is a very dangerous social habit. Ghelerode's innocents are not intelligent, but they are earnest, sincere, and well-wishing. At the worst, they have an amoral sensuality, and a total lack of cruelty at their best—cruelty considered by Ghelerode an intellectual crime.

The denial of rationality in Ghelerode is evident, but his nonrationality does not appear to bring any fruit less bitter. But perhaps Ghelerode is on the side of the angels. Man has allowed himself to forget what religion means—a way of salvation from the devil. We do not have, in this world, so much a ship of fools as we have a ship of destroyed fools. Ghelerode ultimately does not equate the simplicity necessary for salvation with stupidity, but with the instinct that the artist has in seeing to the core of things. Against the truly good heart, Satan cannot prevail.

Chapter 7

Modern Literary Existentialism in England

GRAHAM GREENE

Isolation, pain, suffering and guilt are very much the back-bone of the art of Greene (1904–   ). However, his eschatology involves, as he is a Catholic, the absolute as heaven and hell, sin and punishment, repentance and redemption. If he is an existentialist, he is a Catholic existentialist, and of the variety of Maritain. Thus Greene is one who affirms the "firstness" of the senses and does so in having them posit, finally, the absolutes which we then study from the point of view of the intellect. The Catholic existentialist believes that when essence is wiped out, then existence is necessarily negated. The intellect, willing or not, necessarily comes up with the essence, the absolute idea, the standard, the criterion. Only through essence, asserts Maritain, can we have the affirmation that something exists.

From a purely logical point of view, Maritain's philosophy is impregnable—if the opposition will allow him to set up a completely knowable physical universe which controls and demands qualities and attributes, externally identifiable, of mat-

143

ter. But Greene is not a metaphysician. He does pay much attention to the fact of existence. His own spiritual odyssey demanded an individualism in two ways: as a Protestant, he was an individualist; as a converted Catholic he is caught in the religious arena of a faith that has a central mother, but highly individualistic sons. Greene asserted that he must be true to revealing the emotional state of the individual, and that he must not surrender himself to a collective ideology. The matter of human consciousness interested him most. The nonrational nature of Greene's thought makes it necessary for the intellect to bring into question the support of any group organization. Thus the Church itself is as much under question as Fascism, Nazism, and Marxism. Maritain's existentialism, in the hands of Greene, has been a goad in the side of the orthodox Catholic.

We simply need to know what kind of Christian, nonChristian, agnostic, or atheist we have before us. Greene is a Christian and Catholic existentialist. As an existentialist he will start with himself and, as an individual, he is going to give his consciousness careful consideration with respect to those absolutes outside. He will reach them, in his own terms.

A convert to Catholicism is a source of great uneasiness to both Catholics and Protestants. The very experience that brought Greene to the Catholic religious position involves great questions and soul-searching. Such searching is the kind that well-drilled Catholics never have to encounter. They do not encounter themselves, since their training has been almost below the level of consciousness. The same situation is true of the Methodist. He may be a good Methodist if he obeys Methodist principles, but he never has to hold any other principles up against those of Methodism—since he has not encountered them. If he begins to doubt, at least initially, he doubts within the one Methodist context. The same situation is true of believers in other creeds and religions. Greene could not write an experience about a Catholic who had never been conscious of any other spiritual stimulation, and perhaps never reflectively conscious of that one.

As a novelist, and as a valid one, Greene furnishes the grounds for imagination; he provides the stuff of experience. Now, this material is fictive; by fictive we mean that although the subject may be unreal as to name, event, place, date, and verifiable physical experiences, the theme and thesis are true to some or all aspects of man and are possible to the particular people involved.

Starting with existence in each individual, Greene engrosses the reader with what appears to be melodramatic techniques. In tragedy, revolt is short, destruction certain, and annihilation complete. In melodrama, the unlikely happens; the life is saved; or the soul is saved; or, what is comic, they live happily ever afterward. The public demands the lie of melodrama, the asserted wish that becomes reality. The comedian becomes a tragic figure. A truly tragic figure becomes comic, a sheer impossibility where religion is logical. We come to realize that only one religion is logical, that of the Greeks. Christianity and Judaism are delightfully irrational; therefore, what can make better melodrama than the novel by writers who are conscious of their religious hopes and doubts?

Greene is an excellent novelist in the respect of providing obstacles for his characters to hurdle or on which to destroy themselves. Political clashes, sensuality, perversion, robbery, and crimes of violence are the material of experience. The experiences he presents are so formidable, indeed, that his characters need to agonize, despair, challenge, and defy in order to surmount them. His existentialism, as Catholic, is quite dramatically evident in his ability to create plausible individuals under conditions that seem farfetched. Greene succeeds in this modern tempo through not stopping long for conscious reflection or for long intellectual introspections. He has the quality of the modern existentialist in full degree: he can move through much immediacy of experience in rapid time.

LAURENCE DURRELL

Durrell (1912–   ), born in India, obtained his education in India and at Canterbury, served in the Foreign Office in the Southeast part of Continental Europe. Apart from travel books, children's literature, poetry, he has written novels.

Durrell is the novelist of space and time. He contends that because we have no unity today in life or in literature, literature, at least, should involve a consideration of the dimensions of time and those of volume. He asserts that such dimensions are relative to the individual who makes them as large or as small as he desires on each occasion.

As matter moves in unpredictable random motions at all times, but predictably so as law, and as the three dimensions constituting volume and time circumscribe a world of man, within such a world there are infinite possibilities of combinations. Thus his literary output has been varied; his interests and revelations include sonnets, melodramas, soliloquys, criticism, comedy, journalism, foreign policy, and publicity assignments. Through his characters in the Alexandria Quartet, he presents his concept of life. There are many views of life, as Justine expresses for Durrell. One person presents to the other a different view, another profile. For one situation and for one set of observers there is one part of a multifaceted human being. Experience, then, must be immediate and concrete as having truth. Imagine character A with a certain number of facets, all at a certain time and place. A disturbs the consciousness of B, C, D, and E who are themselves in a certain time and place. That they will always be at the same absolute position is impossible; therefore, they are meaningful to each other only insofar as the next actualized moment in time is concerned. Life is an infinite series of absolutes, but relative to each other over time.

Durrell's philosophy has been presented as being difficult, but one would doubt that he is that troublesome. We might start from the Platonic view, although Durrell would start from the existing individual; in this case, we believe that the result will be the same. If we consider each man as possessing a number of possible qualities which he can make patent under the right conditions, in human relationships, we also consider that of the total number possible, he has a limited number. If we now consider that there are many other individuals who also have a certain number of qualities and characteristics of the total number possible, we will know that each person has some of the qualities possessed by others. Certain basic qualities will be present in each individual and common to each by virtue of being a man, and not some other creature. On the other hand, some will have qualities not possessed by the "other." Finally, the qualities possessed by each will differ in quality—as intensity and strength—from other individuals.

If these people come together in relationships, they will be bound by the relationships that man can have by being a man. Since we are not all at the same place at the same time, we cannot have relationships with all the others. At any one time and place, we can have relationships only with certain people. These relationships will depend upon the physical, emotional, and intellectual states of each person. Because no psychological state will be the same for each, different qualities of the same individuals will also come into play at different experiences as each person actualizes his next second, or his next immediacy of experience. Justine points out that every single picture has some reality, but no one picture is truth. And such must be the case. However, for the one moment and for the qualities interacting there is the truth of that situation—as far as the consciousnesses of the interactants are concerned.

Durrell wants to sort out the images we desire to show and to show the real images that represent the character. But he is defeated in at least one respect: a reality of man as such is that he has a private world that he will not demonstrate to anyone. The novelist cannot be the god who finds that private area because even he stands in his own way.

If Durrell asks that we concede, as an opening position, that if every patent quality of a person could be revealed at one time and could be seen by the observer at one time as that quality was, we would know the reality of the individual, we would have to dissent. We would also have to believe that we know ourselves and all of our qualities as well as we know the other. We have an impossibility here—as Pirandello showed in *Henry IV*. But even if we grant Durrell's position, the statement would be true only for the single experience. We also quarrel with his definition of fiction—or with his nondefinition of fiction. By fiction we understand the literary state wherein the author furnishes grounds for imagination, and reveals the truth of man at the cost of admitting that he cannot verify the physical, intellectual, or emotional truth of the individual he uses for his literary expression. Fiction as false is unsatisfactory because we cannot agree that the author will always know when he is selecting the image to present and when he is not. We cannot know that if he selects an image to present, thinking that image not to be true, that he has not, ironically, presented the true self. If the deliberate presentation of the image one wants believed is a part of the predicament of man, is that not the reality of man and the truth of man? We believe that these speculations must be kept in mind in considering Durrell.

C. P. SNOW

Snow (1905–   ) was born in the provinces, attended Cambridge, served as scientist for the government, became a writer in 1934 with his novel *The Search,* and since the World War II period has produced eight novels under the title *Strangers and Brothers,* name of the first of the series. We consider his works only with respect to what can be considered existential qualities. He is by no means an existentialist: if he were to be classified here analytically, we would consider him in the classical tradition, for he uses the total facts of personality to question and relate to such moral absolutes as honor, duty, and responsibility. The central figure, usually representing Snow, is Lewis Eliot, lawyer and government official. Zealous supporter of ideals and implacable foe of a middle position, he is thwarted by society and economics, and never has a top administrative role. Lewis is a member of the Establishment, a committeeman and one who believes that compromise is an evil only in what meaning the word takes on in America. In the United States, "compromise" has a sinister connotation. The English view is that compromise means that a solution is good, and that no solution is bad, with the agreement that the solution reached by the compromise is a matter of immediacy. Lewis knows what choice means, but he cannot commit society to his own individual point of view.

Snow's main existential quality is that, in compromise, there has been honest assertion; the man must find his identity in the following way: he must choose whatever he chooses so that he is a responsible person, and responsible to himself. When he makes a political decision, for example, the decision must come from himself to the outside. Although he considered himself agnostic, Snow's world has absolutes even though the virtues he admires are more those of Marcus Aurelius and the Greek virtues, rather than those that are Christian. But his existential qualities are marked in his insistence on challenging absolutes, in making the world horizontal, in the emphasis on making one's own choice. We must not be led to believe that merely because the decision of the hero seems to be in favor of accommodation to social issues that there is no commitment. The commitment is entirely personal.

WILLIAM GOLDING

Golding (1911–   ) was educated at Oxford, was a school teacher for many years, and was a lecturer at Hollins College in Virginia. His qualities are those of the writer of allegory, the religious thinker, the isolated and sensitive individual, and the mind seized with the capacity for evil, guilt, and suffering. His faith in the intellect is limited, and he believes that an irrational world only could give man a consciousness with which to torment and be tormented. Specific qualities derive from these basic characteristics of his art. *Pincher Martin* reveals man's suffering through his reason. Pincher fought only for his identity. Sartre would consider this an example of good faith, living and dying by what he knows himself to be, not what he would be. Nevertheless, Golding moves to the existential positions, but does so as a Christian, almost in the Maritain tradition and position. Man starts with his existence to move himself to God, as essential, demanding, and moral. Golding accuses Martin of not accepting the annihilation of self, for dying. Thus, we have Golding as a religious existentialist, for Martin's was the choice to die for his identity, or to use his identity as existing, his death for God.

SAMUEL BECKETT

Born in Ireland in 1906 and educated in Ireland at Trinity College, Beckett went to France in 1922 as a lecturer in English. He returned to Ireland for a short time, during which period he acquired his master of art's degree from Trinity College. After some time in France and Germany, Beckett worked for James Joyce. He took up permanent residence in France and made French his official language.

The key note in Beckett is pessimism; but comedy has always been a matter of pessimism. Man suffers from both illusions and delusions, and probably suffers equally severely from each. His most significant quality is his intellectualization that the intellect is inadequate, utterly. Man can gain no truth by systematic thinking; whatever truth there is, will not be derived by man's conceptualizations. Yet by conceptualization does Beckett make the statement.

How does Beckett claim that truth does not exist? He states that truth is not susceptible to human intellect, but that truth is an ultimate matter to which man does not, by any faculty he possesses, have access. Beckett is pushing his pessimism to its opposite—optimism. Plato would probably have agreed that the ultimate truth is not accessible to the mind, but he would have added that there is much more available to the mind than to either the will or the world of matter. What bothers Beckett is that knowing *about* truth is possible, as rational, but that knowing truth itself is not. He would not face any opposition on that score from the church and from the majority of philsophical thinkers. When we consider the existential views, we can see that much despair comes from minds that are artistic in nature. The artist has always had difficulty with man's institutional strictures: in this age, with its materialism, the outside regulations are even more onerous. Although man has always had difficulty in making peace between his individual claims and with those of society, the sheer weight of the number of outside rules and regulations has increased almost geometrically. What he cannot cope with seems to present either a dead person, a dead weight of outside reality, or both. Not being able to cope with the relationship of individual to outside world, the artist and writer try to establish all the world that is needed within the individual. But such a world is often cast in the same language—oral or written—or rationally reconstituted as that which governs the outside society.

The individual then seeks a reality in and within himself through emotional states, physical sensations, or introspections, all derived from the inside and projected back onto the consciousness, or projected out upon the outside world. Highly sensitive individuals like Beckett, Genet, Camus, Sartre, Giraudoux, and the others we have discussed, all suffer traumatic blows to the entire personality, primarily because their intellectual powers are not adequate. Yet, ironically, these intellectual powers are their greatest asset. For all their deprecation of the intellect, they are highly cerebral. Beckett, perhaps, is more cerebral than the others; therefore his distress is greater when he finds inadequate support from an intellectual position. Beckett finds that his keenest intellectual insights serve but to reveal opposition of one idea to another. Knowledge is an illusion, Beckett would say. We collapse when we face religion because we can find no support for its position. Not many people like missionaries, and we can believe that not many missionaries care too much for those being "missionaried." The "ing" is more attractive than its object. Such people as Beckett become dismayed when not all the horrible and rejected members of society want to be converted to the existential point of view. The existentialists prove their own paradox because even though they consider society as nothingness, indeed they insist on audiences, play to audiences, and write about audiences.

As Genet would hold, there must be a belief to knock down. For him, who has placed everything in one intellectual "egg basket," having tossed away materiality and the will, there must be complete nothingness—which by the principle of opposition, he pushed into quite a bit of something. If he does not furnish something for himself, his *Waiting for Godot* has brought many writers and theories back to life.

There is general agreement that the play is about "waiting" and not about Godot. Man's individual human condition is such that even though he denies the external world of mind, body, and spirit, and even though he denies his own, he cannot avoid waiting. Waiting for whom or what is not the human crisis, but the waiting itself. Beckett drives home one concept clearly: in a traditional sense man is confronted with clock time, God's time (eternal time), and psychological time. These pose no difficulty to the understanding: clock time measures the intervals in physical change; eternal time is that comprehension or experience of being close to, or apart from, a spiritual heaven or hell in traditional statements.

ANGUS WILSON

Wilson (1913–   ) lived in South Africa, moved to England, and attended Westminster and Oxford. He served during the war at the Foreign Office and then occupied himself as librarian at the British Museum. He decided to quit to devote himself to writing.

Wilson has quite a range of satire, a tremendous depth of feeling, a sense of evil, a despair at work not completed, and the feeling of inadequacy of the liberal mind in this current world. Among Wilson's ideas are the theses that people are always comic, and that they prefer their delusions to the truth.

People as to stated creeds and personal conduct differ radically: X can live with Y if each can delude the other. In any combat between youth and middle-age, where truth is involved, the middle-aged person is destroyed. He who stays with vice is destroyed, not the one symbolizing vice. Humanity, liberality, and charity cannot contend with social mores, militarism, and materiality. Viciousness is a part of the human predicament, a predicament which is basically one of evil.

People do not solve their problems by understanding each other; the problems remain, but the reasons for suffering are clearer. Everyone is a fool: some people are more foolish than others, and there are different kinds of fools.

ALAN SILLITOE

Sillitoe (1928–   ) was born in Nottingham and lived in its slums until he left to make bicycles. Following a stint in the RAF, he married an American girl and lived for a time in Majorca.

From *The Loneliness of the Long-Distance Runner* come the following thoughts:

1. A man must be what he is, not what he would like to be. He must have good faith. In *The Loneliness of the Long-Distance Runner* the hero has to make a decision. Shall he stay with those opposed to the law and lose the race, or shall he give in and win because of better treatment than his friends receive? He asserts his identity and loses. He obeys the law of his jungle. (We have here a version of the

underworld code in which a dying man will refuse to identify his assassins.)

2. The world consists of two jungles: the "we" jungle against the "they" jungle. There is no compromise between the two.

3. No man can afford to live according to an external image unless he does so in the knowledge that he is making a conscious choice outside himself. He cannot follow an external stereotype and be free.

4. The enemy is more to be respected than the one who tries to temporize or to take up a position between the pursuers and the pursued.

5. Facing the limitations that must result when the minority are assailed by or assail the majority, the individual must commit himself to himself, no matter what side he is allied with. He is free only insofar as he decides and exists himself.

KINGSLEY AMIS

Amis (1922–   ) pursues, with Fieldian humor, man's search for identity and man's dread of facing the world whose changes have been so great that any idea of making a smooth transition seems impossible. The gulf between what his people find the world to be and their own visions of themselves as adequate or inadequate are worlds apart. The comic fracturing of the Queen's English is in keeping with the world they attempt. Despite the comic festival, the basic terms of life are never far away. The somber, ruthless, and brutal tone of Sillitoe is not obvious in Amis' literature, but the comic notes are only too close to pessimism.

Writers of the tradition of romantic naturalism and existential qualities use colors symbolically. Amis uses colors not as a distraction, but as quick symbolization of the character—for example, colors which range from red, orange, yellow, green

. . . black range downward from warmth and passion to austerity in emotion. Orange-red, rather than reddish-orange, is significant.

Amis' heroes have existential qualities, for each insists on existing himself part way. Like Malamud and Bellow, however, Amis' characters accommodate themselves, even though they enter the world of dreams and fancies. At this point of accommodation, we find the gulf between being existential and being an existentialist. The existential emphases in these novels come in making a decision as to which world to accommodate in from a position starting with the self. However, existentialism collapses when the existing position leads to externals which inevitably do the choosing, rather than being chosen.

JOHN WAIN

Wain (1925–) was born in Staffordshire, educated at Oxford, lectured at Reading University, and left to write novels.

Wain's idiom is rougher, harder-hitting, and more moral than the comic spirit of Amis. His hero in *Hurry on Down* (1953) is certainly a hero of reduced limits, but he has a wide range of experiences: cleaner, smuggler of narcotics, driver, comic writer and bouncer. Like the heroes of Amis, Wain's central figure has usually graduated from a university which he despises for its lack of meaning. He wants his own identity, which he can achieve only through avoiding being caught at what a university man would usually be doing. But he has problems, too. In the conventionally low pursuits he follows, he does not want to be identified with the lower class. He wants to be himself. He finds that the absurdity of the world is its identification of people by what calling they pursue, or by what external functions they perform.

Charles Lumley, the protagonist, finds that the people in the world do identify people by what they do and that they ought to do what they are trained to do. Those who catch Charles at his nonacademic jobs castigate and damn him completely. He is not playing the game, not playing cricket. Our hero is frustrated at every turn. Whatever he does brings him into contact with a force that is real, powerful in all its aspects—society. When he smuggles dope, all society is identified, and he is identified by all society.

A Travelling Woman (1959) produces another indication of the fact that the existential man can run: we have another version of the "rabbit." Even admitting that modern mobility makes for running, Wain's runners go beyond the usual concepts of being transient. His runners have as much of the "rabbit" in them as Updike, the American writer, has in his work *Rabbit, Run*.

The hero is George Links. A married man, he shows some imagination as, fed up with his wife, he seeks the aid of a psychiatrist, but the aid is not the expected kind. The character Captax has fooled himself in the comic tradition in believing that George's wife is an external symbol of a great love to which he can commit himself. But betrayal intervenes, and each finds himself committed to betrayal, rather than to the flesh and blood creature he needs. George realizes that he would rather be bored with one total commitment to his wife than to be betrayed by his own betrayal. He would rather pledge his faith and his entire self to "loving" his wife than to loving his betrayal of his own wife and two other people.

There are two objections at this point. The characters are not worth saving since each has completely betrayed the other. Each does not return to love, but rather returns because the first choice was better than the second. We cannot call the story immoral because innocence has not been smirched. From the comic point of view, each deserves the other, and there is little merit. But they are human beings, and, being conscious of guilt, there is always the chance that they may accept responsibility for good.

The other puzzle has to do with loyalty and faith. The very intellectualization of the entire business excludes "faith" from the discussion as having any useful meaning. Loyalty can exist only once; Sartre pointed that out in his discussion of "bad faith." There is no such thing as a "loyal traitor."

JOHN BOWEN

Bowen (1924–   ) was born in India, graduated from Oxford and studied in America.

Bowen's sojourn in America directed him toward American themes and terms, but his work is more universal than restricted to either England or America. Social justice, satire, hypocrisies, and all values that are set and fixed are under attack. Beneath his naturalism as technique, his soul is the existential soul that is alienated, isolated, and deprived as any soul must be that views the world honestly.

The Truth Will Not Help Us (1956) goes back in history—as Miller went back in *The Crucible*—to attack "investigations" and witch hunts. In 1705 three English sailors are unjustly hanged, and hanged in the name of a meaningless concept of piracy. The sailors are assured they are not under trial, but the investigation convicts them, and does so by "guilt by association." To gain universality—as Shakespeare did—Bowen relies on anachronism. Thus the 1705 scene is larded with all the paraphernalia of mass media. We have the official who never desires to have anyone disturb the small official universe. No one must rock the boat. Those who should defend the aliens find pressure of other affairs. From a moment of neutrality, the press builds up situations whereby the townspeople come to believe that they have desperate characters with them. Aliens have intruded themselves in lawless acts; seamen are drifters bringing evil to the town. They are not settled in their ways, and have no property, no settled community.

By the time the trial has come, the men are virtually convicted, and the screams of the bloodthirsty, vicious, and sadistic middle and lower class who have a desire for blood are let loose.

In a rough way, there are Durrell's notes, the questions of seeing what we want to see and of false identity. The moment man permits any slogan or "ism" to be set up as absolute, individual integrity and choice fail.

NORMAN F. SIMPSON

Simpson (1919–   ) gives attention to England's middle-class citizens, and does so in projecting a strong realism into fantasy. His *modus operandi* is to take a common situation, A, and present the entire situation in a full context, indicating the ridiculousness and absurdity in life and people. If man is absurd in his old social environment and cannot tell that he is absurd, showing his ridiculousness in a new environment might get the point across. However, there is danger in such a situation, and Simpson has not entirely avoided the danger. The critics may not see that man is absurd in the old A, but only that he is absurd when thrown into B; when such occurs, the critic and audience are more likely to be offended than enlightened. We must hope that the character who does not know what the world is all about in A will be enlightened in B, with respect to both A and B.

A Resounding Tinkle (1957) indicates that part of Simpson's problem is that of naturalism. He is concerned with

man's inability to use a highly developed intellect to create a
true picture of the world and his relationship to its environment. He decries man's use of religion to support the universe
he constructs for himself through his intellect. If man can have
no knowledge of reality, then is not nature playing a Homeric
joke on him? Is he not the toy of the world of matter and its
laws? If human intellect serves no purpose, and if all of his
material and cultural efforts, resulting mainly from development of the nervous system, are to no avail, then man must be
lost. Reason, as useless as its results appear to be, is the best that
man can offer his universe.

There is no question that this position has to be one of despair, dread, anguish, and dismay. Then why is Simpson so
completely given over to the comic roars of unrestrained laughter? We believe that such gargantuan hilarity can come only
from the human mind in complete despair. Careful attention
to all the words of the comedians and to the prayer and its
response will reveal that there is no solution other than laughter, because whatever man does and whatever he thinks of as
his own unique faculty and bit of worth are but phenomena of
nature, beyond explanation or explication. The absurdity is in
trying to provide sane explanations for a world of matter
whose irrational flow of matter is the only dark divinity. We
do not have the existential mind dominant in this play. The
opposition in words—*Resounding Tinkle*—indicates that as far
as nature is concerned, the thunder of man in his own ears is
truly but a microcosmic tinkle. Beyond despair, there is hilarity, and one can laugh at the code, but live with the code, insofar as man knows that his construction of his universe can be
changed to any other construction as far as he measures his life
against the grim relentlessness of a ceaseless, random, and re-
morseless flow of atoms. Getting over the bitter taste of being a

nonentity, Simpson drops in and out of the play. He has already warned the audience of the breaks in the play, of the interruptions. He is never more serious than when he is nonsensical, for his very pattern of breaking the experience up into fragments parallels the discontinuity of matter. The elephant in the play has several connotations, but the most common in the mythical sense is the symbol of being powerful in an irrational nature. Thus, the elephant must go because the concept of nature herself as god is too much for suburbia. The snake has varied meanings, but Blavatsky and Diel postulate the snake as standing for seduction of strength by matter, inferior elements in a superior entity, and evil in things classified as wordly. Whether evil is introduced by man's postulation of himself as superior to and the conqueror of nature, or whether nature herself is evil and all-embracive is paradoxical, as are the Paradocks. The drinking of the nectar of the gods is not absurd if nature herself is god—as in naturalism—because the gods would be as absurd as man, and would be so in more intense degrees. If nature herself provides the illusion discussed in the prayer-response situation, then all of nature is evil, and one reality is not more ridiculous than another. If we consider this point carefully, we can understand the existential revolt.

The Hole brings a philosopher to the scene. A group is gathered around a hole—as crowds in a city will stand and watch people digging a hole for a building foundation. This hole, however, is deep and dark, and metaphysical speculations are being made as to its nature, while some other speculations are not so metaphysical. A philosophical mystic, who behaves as though he were trying to be the spirit in the hub of the philosopher's, wheel, holds forth on what is taking place in the hole. The mystic believes that a religious event must occur. Religious events are anathema to naturalism, since nature herself is completely autonomous as god. As person after person comes by, each gives his ten cents worth of intellectual speculation to the unfathomable hole. Here we have the existential "filling-in." In the discussions that ensue, every form of human activity and interest is covered. As time goes on, the speculations become wilder and more violent. At the moment of highest confusion, a simple worker tells everyone that the hole holds a unit storage box of electrical energy. If we are alert, we will react to this "electrical" stimulus because scientists consider that the stream of electrons—negative particles of electricity—are of the very basic stuff of life.

HAROLD PINTER

Pinter, a member of the "absurd" fraternity, was born in 1930. His early experiences include writing poetry, acting, and attempting to write a novel. He started to write plays when he was twenty-seven. His first play is unique neither to the existential mind nor to the tradition of the absurd. *The Room* (1957) has shadings of French existentialism and of the absurdity in Ionesco and Genet. Pinter is not as direct as Ionesco or Genet, and not as subtle as Beckett. He has certain qualities, however, that make him unique, despite his heritage from other playwrights.

The Room (1957) has a straightforward framework. Two people, a husband and wife, are in a room; there is speculation on what will happen if the room is entered from without. The two know that they are safe within; they are terror-stricken concerning what may lurk outside. Because we have two people, we have a real relationship. Stream of consciousness is more tolerable and more easily assimilated when two people are present because there is little possibility that they can long remain oblivious to each other. To make the connection more realistic, we find that although the husband wastes no words on the wife, there is communication to the extent that he is made much of and grossly catered to by his wife Rose. The old wife and old husband do not know the old landlord; Rose is not conscious of her own physical surroundings. In fact, neither one is conscious of more than the nearest physical objects circumscribing the limited world in which each lives; by extension, no one is any more awake.

By the arrival of a Negro, the intimacy has been penetrated; thus the light within the room goes out. The Negro is traditionally symbolic as the child of darkness. Therefore, his intrusion into the room must throw the couple into darkness. Their light is broken by intrusion, and his darkness must not be borne by her.

JOHN OSBORNE

Osborne (1930–   ) was born in London, and educated until he was expelled from school at sixteen. He trained hard as an actor, then as a playwright. Osborne's principal qualities are his ability to strike the universal theme and to make his fury and anger sound real. Attached to no school, expelled from one, and fighting his way from the obscurity of provincial acting, he had the audacity to stand out against the mild observers and to thunder his challenge. Emotionalism should be felt, so Osborne did not lose his force in having an object for most of his objections. He looked about and he looked back, and he started being angry, being furious, and saying something about the miserable rot of a man in British society. He made the gerundial attack, a "general annihilating."

Osborne did not intend to lead a revolt; to do so would make revolt an object and put himself in a position of being linked with the object of his attack. He spoke from his own outraged consciousness.

In *Look Back in Anger* Jimmy Porter has neither a particular object he dislikes nor any reform he wants to lead. He is unhappy with his frustrated condition. The entire world is absurd; there would be no point in singling out one adversary; the whole universe crushes him. He sags beneath the weight of its rot. In an era when we would rather talk than fight, Jimmy can "natter" with the best of them. He has graduated from the university; instead of trying to accommodate—as the British novelists were urging—Jimmy is screaming from something within himself that is wrong. There is the world and Jimmy; his consciousness and what is outside are not in tune; there is interference. He does not see the force that is possessing, but he feels its pressures.

Osborne's controversial play *Luther* is quite in keeping with his existential bias, as well as that of Luther. Osborne's intent was to put the figure of Luther on a realistic plane, to make him a human and suffering individual. The many references to the realistic but less refined aspects of human anatomy are not without precedent. While one admires a Swift, he seldom loves him, particularly if he has a weak stomach or a sensitive cultural receiving center. The difference here is that Swift did not put his material on the stage in one concentrated purgative to a group of thin-skinned people in a thin-skinned age or in the atmosphere of a welfare state. One can read Swift a while and close the book. But bowels, intestines, fleas, boils, and all unseemly forms of human excrescence beat, from the stage, on one's ears, causing a Sartrian nausea.

Nausea is particularly acceptable to the existentialist, especially to the continental variety. But there are not many existentialists in the Anglo-English audiences. Nausea makes for dramatic physical reactions, but not for much intellectual stimulation. As Tennyson pointed out, we are not what we once were, but discussing the birth of a new religion as an evacuation is not only questionable as to taste, but also as to valid analogy. However, Osborne is not without profound truth; the Renaissance personality, for all of his intellectual vigor and for all of his emotive zest, was not without powerful bent to the world of the stimulating senses. The Renaissance individual, furthermore, was not alien to suffering, nor averse to suffering. "Be my joy three parts pain" was as real to Luther as to Crashaw. The play has powerful existential notes.

ARNOLD WESKER

Wesker (1932–   ), born in the East End of London, worked as a plumber and as a pastry cook—he was a good one. He became interested in films, and studied at the London School of Film Technique.

Wesker in drama, like Snow in the novel, traces central figures. Wesker takes a situation involving a Jewish family and its communist members. The time spanned is twenty-three years, commencing in 1936. As in Brechtian art, there are verifiable historical events. The strong group sociological patterns prepare the audience and reader for propaganda. Wesker, like Osborne, is able to make the problem universal, and Wesker's achievement is the more remarkable for his single family. But he has a spread of years to help him. The family is the Kahns, and the transposition of a letter will make the name significant.

BRENDAN BEHAN

Behan (1923–1964), who died from alcoholism (as did Dylan Thomas), and who won fame in England and more in America, wrote two significant plays that represent a borderline membership in the Theatre of the Absurd. Behan found the world so absurd that he drank his way out. Despite the fact that he had been imprisoned for nine years for crimes no worse than being an Irish nationalist, his plays show no violent bitterness at his personal suffering. Man should, if anything, sympathize because we are together in a rough and senseless world. His two plays—*The Quare Fellow* (1945) and *The Hostage* (1957)—oppose only hypocrisy and morality set out in abstractions: sham and hypocrisy make the world ridiculous and unbearable.

The Quare Fellow is the name given to any person who is to be hanged. No matter how long these Irish prisoners are in jail and irrespective of their previous violence, which has been unlimited, they are shaken by an execution evening. One absurdity is that the audience never sees the victim, but all that is known is deduced from the conduct of the prisoners who feel caught up in a hostile world.

In *The Hostage,* despite its humor, the meaning strikes deeply. No one really understands what is going on. A boy who should be at school is challenging the English over a cause he could not describe and fighting for a cause whose name he could not probably read or write. The British believe that hanging a man, a boy, will dry up the wellsprings of nationalism. The wild IRA officer is absurd in believing that the British government will pay blackmail for any life, particularly that of a private soldier. The absurdity of running a house of prostitution ceases being absurd when we realize that all de-cent values have been prostituted. What is absurd is that Theresa, an innocent, should be in the house. The awesome absurdity is revealed when we find that innocence can be destructive. Unwittingly she brings the boy's death upon him; yet she will know and not know. Ironically, when the police come, they do not come for the hostage, but to investigate vice charges. There is vice, but not the kind they seek: the vice is the entire human predicament. The homosexuals, as absurdly, turn out to be vice-squad detectives.

IRIS MURDOCH

Murdoch (1919–　) was born in Dublin, educated at Oxford, worked for the British Treasury during World War II, married John Bayley, and currently teaches at Oxford.

Under the Net (1954) is a search for identity, but a subtle one, for Murdoch's brilliant but totally undisciplined art covers a tremendous range. How does one find the right life? Donaghue is the hero of this novel, one set in the seamier parts of London and Paris. If a man plans his activity, there is no guarantee that he can make the thing work as he wants it to. Looking for a way out, Jake is always under the net, since rationality, contrary to Wilson's position, does not work. The author uses various kinds of symbolism from animate objects to gardens. The garden represents the spirit of truth, the tenderness of all creation at its core. Only through instinct and intuition can one drive to its meaning. Jake, "out of his water," pursues his ideal love through the garden, but fails because he is lost. For him, the garden is illusionary, and, finally, "nothingness." All that counts is man's desperate attempt to define himself, to find an identity he can live with. Jake points out that rationality and theory are of little avail. Like the practical mother in *The Lady's Not For Burning,* only the one situation at one time counts. Jake has pursued the intellect and the will, but finally finds a concrete position. Jake, in his irrationality, steals, cunningly, Mars, a film-featured canine. The dog symbolizes valor, guardian and companion of the dead. He wants to exchange the dog for a lost manuscript. But no one wants the dog back. Whatever value he represented at one time has gone. The past has no meaning—a good existential position.

In all of Murdoch's novels there are forms of old Tiresias— the ones who know all or see all. But she, like Sartre, is going to crush any hope for a supreme external being. In *The Flight from the Enchanter* (1956) the characters turn to Peter for advice. No answer that is given is ever transcendentally correct. One of two instances are developed: first, the advice is faulty and flawed; second, the character does not understand what he is told.

The Sandcastle (1957) has a title highly suggestive of a message of instability. We have a siege between intellect and art coming up for review. The hero, Mor, is forty-plus—and a schoolteacher; the heroine is Rain, the young artist. They attempt a love union, but one doomed to fail because it is planned. The ingredients are present: sand and rain. But the sand is not the right kind, and there is too much or too little rain. The forced union can not endure. The Sartrian concept of freedom is present in this novel. The concept of bad faith is also present. So is the animal. In tying these together, we find that Mor's wife Nan, Felicity, and her brother are on one side of the tug-of-war, and that Mor and his freedom are on the other side. The dog is dead, but in the minds of Mor and the other members of the family, he represents loyalty and watchfulness. But that is the past, not the present, but the past in the consciousness of each actualized future as present. Thus the dead hand of the past comes to each future moment to bar freedom.

Iris Murdoch's *The Unicorn* (1963) turns on the symbol itself. The unicorn is the symbol of chastity and also of the sword which refers to the word of God. No one can capture the unicorn when in pursuit, but when a virgin approaches, the unicorn kneels in complete submission. Many authorities hold that such a phenomenon of kneeling before the virgin symbolizes sex that has been sublimated. On the other hand, the unicorn also symbolizes evil toward man. Myth associates a white body, red head, and blue eyes with this animal. In *The Flight from the Enchanter* there is the crystalline light (as white) and blue and red metallic flowers, in Mischa Fox's house, the house of the enchanter. Here we have the unicorn symbol, with evil toward men and submission to a virgin—but not to nonvirgins.

Chapter 8

■

Modern Literary Existentialism in the United States

Introductory

The forces that have given rise to the problems of self as reflected in English and Continental literature have also concerned America. Although we are much closer together through greater publishing volume, through wider reading, through mass transportation improvement, through the increased personal contacts with people of other countries, and through continual exposure to all mass media, the United States invariably catches the literary and philosophical movements after they have waned in France and England particularly. Naturalism entered its death throes and agonies in the immediate postwar (World War II) period. American scholars have outworn even more the already outworn thesis of Hemingway and Steinbeck. While the researchers are going back for a third try, new and significant literature is under way. We state a historical fact; very little can be done about appreciating literature of the immediate present; we must stand some years away. However, we can look at the French and English literature, knowing that before long we shall see its presence in America. More competent and more immediate translations, and subsidies for having foreign works translated for the public, enable the American public to experience European thought more directly and more immediately than was formerly the case. TV programs, guest lectures, and cultural exchange of artists and teachers also are making for the improved transfers of ideas and ideals.

United with a thoroughgoing naturalism, whose violence is entirely acceptable to us because we are a violent people, was also an expressionism strongly grounded in violence. We have also adopted and adapted ourselves to Freudianism with more wholehearted enthusiasm than other countries. Because of our tendency to divide the standard and not its object, and because of our further tendency to talk in terms of extremes (thrifty —spendthrift; white—black; theoretical—practical, among others), our naturalism and expressionism have been very grim without being subtle. But naturalism is an impossible creed to endure for long. The atomic bomb and its effects have been wrongly interpreted as a manifestation of nature. Because nature herself is God in naturalism, we have found that a philosophy of life based upon naturalism causes and demands such an external negative code (e.g., Hemingway) that few people can or will live through its tenets. Pirandello, Betti, Ghelerode, and the angry young men of England turned aside from its strictures. Suicide, an increased incidence of mental disturbance, alcoholism, and drug addiction as results of naturalism are particularly objectionable to a people primarily pragmatic.

American letters have rebelled against any totalitarian form of government, but they have been particularly opposed to individualism that directs Nazism and Fascism. Because many of our prominent writers today are Jewish, and because of their necessary reaction to Nazi contempt for the subordinate individual and all individuals' subordination to the state, these writers are inclined to tolerate more leftism and to endure the totalitarianism inherent in Communism while attacking the German, Spanish, and Italian type. That in time the same attack will be delivered on any kind of totalitarianism seems likely. However, they are far more vocal and emotional in their attacks on the right wing than on the left. Marx will be heard where John Birch is anathema. However, careful reading will reveal that the brilliant, if neurotic, line of Jewish spokesmen, are increasingly philosophic—as religious or as atheistic existentialists. In a state that seems increasingly group-minded, such writers as Bellow, Goldman, and Gold, for example, keep individualism alive. Art and culture cannot persist and exist in a group-mind society: he may worship together, but man thinks and creates alone. Many of the middle-class characters treated by Bellow, Goldman, and Gold are seamy and doubtful specimens indeed, and we are fortunate enough that the majority of people are not like them, but these writers do indicate how significant the consciousness of any man can be. They also indicate that we can well look at traditional values that have not met the measure of these intelligent, if decadent, people. We see that they have accepted at least one thesis of naturalism—an alien universe. That they make the universe a personality, and a hostile one, indicates the difference between the scientist and the writer of fiction. On the positive side, careful study of their works will indicate, beyond doubt, that they make sexuality not the cause of moral blight, but the result. The position is, on its face, anti-Puritan. However, as positive as the expressions of our new writers are on the importance of individual consciousness and its inherent worth, and as significant as the expressions of these artists are on the curse of authoritarianism, they have that Hebraic and anti-Hellenic strain that is, by itself, the curse of art, if not the ineradicable blight on art. By Hebraic we mean the Hebraic-Christian way of looking at the world as *becoming,* as the place for right acting, and as the place for strictness of conscience. Using Matthew Arnold's position and definition as to Hellenism, we think of spontaneity of consciousness and of a life seized with right thinking and joyous thinking. The Hebraic concept of viewing the world and virtue as matters of "becoming" is in opposition to the Greek or Hellenic view that we are not in the process of "becoming," we "are." We are complete; we are all that we can be. We cannot become more perfect; we are what we are. But we can discover more perfection, and, in so doing, seize life with "sweetness and light."

For those who have been waiting and waiting an interminably long time for Hellenism to leaven the Hebraism made official by the Puritans and "improved" upon by a long and weary succession of our writers—including Poe—there is dismay.

We are not concerned with the forerunners who made writing and free expression possible for Bellow and Malamud as far as existentialism is concerned. Those forerunners were too busy freeing the human spirit from gross oppression and physically enforced alienation and solitude to be seized with the alienation of man from himself. West, Rosenfeld, Trilling, Roth, Schwartz, and Kaplan have been occupied with setting man free so that other writers can find a place in which to be isolated.

Irwin Shaw and Herman Wouk are romantic naturalism's most significant—and most prosperous—Jewish-American writers. We would do well to consider, in review, three groups of these novelists and short story writers. First, we have the group, cited earlier, which fought the Depression, narrow

American prejudice, economic and social injustice, and authoritarianism. We have a continuation of the group that battled during pre-World War II days—some of the members not the contemporaries of Bellow—and this second group has had the difficult task of rejecting the left, rejecting the right, freeing itself from the taint of being associated with Communism in various witch hunts, and still trying to find enough creativity left for artistic expression. The dramatist Arthur Miller is a classic example of the plight of the group, as witness *The Crucible*. The third group includes the writers whose members spice up Hemingway's naturalism with romantic ironies and protests against social injustice, well-spiced with well-spaced sensuality.

Henry James stood, and stands, until the present moment, as the bulwark of this Hebraism: Hail to the American and English—strong of moral stature and culturally as sterile and barren as any desert! But our new writers completely submerge Hellenism to the point where not even the faintest ray can play upon experience. Although we have been told by the writers in the tradition of naturalism that our joy is more than likely to be the standard three parts pain, we have arbitrarily removed aesthetic pleasure except for the grotesque kind. The very protest against morality indicates their agonizing concern over its absence. They confuse being absent with "nonexistence." The very intensity with which they push the spirit toward nihilism is a promise of having Hebraism become Hellenism, for the existential personage that can create darkness and death from and in his consciousness will also be able to—and will—create a world in which he can live and for which he can live.

Bellow, Gold, Goldman, Updike, Kerouac, Ellison, Malamud, Baldwin, and others are in the vanguard, trying to come to grips with an awesome world. Rather than adhere to a passive code, man takes a more positive view toward existence even if to stand out he has to "sit down" or "sit in." The American writer is wearied of trying to adjust, for the *n*th time, to essential man in a world which is both nearer and farther away, and both increasingly huge and minute at the same time. Therefore the writer is constructing a new man, one in terms of man's own consciousness of self.

Why do we have such gloomy notes when the writer tosses away many centuries of development that have made the essential man? Because the writer has set up new standards depending upon only the existent individual, why he should not be happier is apparently a baffling mystery. If he is going to be destroyed, at least he should have the pleasure of being his own problem-setter. If he believes that he can have no more agony than he already has had when adopting traditional standards, why is he so glum and despairing when he sets his own?

Prior to the contemporary scene, his standards were set for him. If they were imposed upon him, at least he could back off and consider them. If he failed in the world of everyday realization of mind, body, and spirit, he could always place the blame on society, the world of the supernatural, and on the material environment of man. With his painful kneeling to Nature herself as god, he could only blame Nature, not mind and spirit; but at least he had one external "goat" to hang life's failures on. Now, having rejected Hemingway *et al.,* he has only one god to whom he can turn, only one standard to which he can refer for judgment: himself. Cut off from all traditional values, alienated from the world of the classic synthesis of mind, spirit, and body, further cut off by denying spirit and intellect, he is reduced to a world of physical sensations. He saves himself from the naturalism inherent in a reversion to a primitive world of grunts and groans only by going to his own consciousness. Many writers turn to sexuality on the grounds that the sensation of sexuality is the most immediate experience that the consciousness can affirm. The affirmation is never to the outside—only to the self. The communication is self-communication. But the writers come to realize that there must be experience for fodder. Experience involves human beings. Since A and B do not react in terms of a traditional standard C, then A and B must react on each other, or possess each other. Because the emphasis is on the individual standard of the individual, the only truth that exists is that he exists. Therefore, for the consciousness of A, we have B, D, E, F, G . . . existing only through and for the consciousness of A. In naturalism, with its grimness, there was some organization against a common enemy. With Nature the villain, A, B, C, D . . . joined in a common code to live on terms with Nature.

Because there is no common external enemy or friend, the individual rends the "other" or the self. He commits sadism and masochism, because through the consciousness of such acting he can become aware of himself and of consciousness, if only through an acting that is confirmed in sensation. Thus, in American writing we have the sadism and masochism of countless robberies, assaults, mayhems, and murders. Where the European will commit the crimes in a symbolic act, we insist upon, and get, the real crime. The individual finds that when he goes to the self, he also has to deal with his own personal devils—there is no other place for them to go, and he cannot shift them on to anyone else. Thus, these modern American writers find agony, despair, isolation, and pain a very real and literal experience, indeed. Denying, if not ignoring external nature, abolishing the supernatural, and shunting aside the intellect that creates external standards, the modern man walks as independent. But he is distressed, with more hell in himself than he desires to bear.

We shall consider William Faulkner first in our review of significant contemporary novelists, and then follow with Norman Mailer. Each has existential qualities, and each has strong, very strong, elements of naturalism. Then we shall follow with a substantial list of authors, and, where applicable, a limited number of playwrights, since there are few playwrights of the existential makeup in this country.

WILLIAM FAULKNER

Faulkner (1897–1962) must be considered a romantic naturalist, or a disciple of naturalism with a romantic overcast. Running along with naturalism for a while, as we have stressed, we find the existential qualities. There is a collective self in his novel: the South. The self is divided, as is the existential self—only the South is treated as a sick individual. There is the decadent side, the cultural side, the spiritual side. Then we have the sick materialism of the current South, the kind represented by the Snopses. There is a sickness "unto death." But the agonies are still violent. The South is, in Faulkner's view, conscious of its own consciousness. Because of Faulkner's struggles to maintain a Protestant eschatology against the encroaching naturalism of the Snopses, and the decadent irrationalism of the aristocrats, Faulkner cannot be said to be an existentialist, as such.

Both naturalism and existentialism travel with the same arsenal: sensuality, the cruelty of sadism and masochism, and a dark view of the alien divinity, Nature. Faulkner does not so much reflect that Nature destroys individuals outright, as that she makes them twisted and deformed. There is the collective consciousness of guilt in the South and in the divided parts of the South, but the guilt is mainly that of the old South, because much of the new South is amoral, a point that troubled Faulkner more than immorality did. Ghelerode, as we noted in some detail, shows twisted and deformed human beings, but his are twisted and deformed through the direct presence of Satan; nevertheless, each has the existential quality of showing what happens to consciousness. Faulkner falls short of obtaining his degree in existentialism because he uses the individual's consciousness to represent an external group or force, each contemporary. With Faulkner, selfhood is suffering because of its failure to commit itself effectively to the force represented—in the aristocrats' case. Selfhood does not develop in the Snopses because of their basic amorality, which ensures that materialism in its concrete forms exists.

As is true with both Ghelerode and Betti, Faulkner is a regionalist who managed to evoke the universal from his narrower geographical setting. Faulkner was not overtly concerned in his novels with economics or politics. In order to indicate the fractured spirit of the South, he used stream-of-consciousness technique, with its fractured fragments and with its inverted and distorted word order. The scene of much of the Faulkner material is aptly named: Yoknapatawpha County—the meaning of the Indiana name is "split land." The split is the heart of Faulkner's concern for and with the South. We consider some of Faulkner's qualities and literary attributes and assertions:

1. The Old Southern code stressed honor, decency, generosity, and graciousness.

2. The aristocracy exercised a paternal condescension to the Negroes.

3. The other white people were not worthy of the code.

4. The South lost because there was not enough of the code to spread around, and because the moral code also needed pity and honor.

5. The old order was weakened by lack of stamina.

6. The old order was not good enough, but modern materialism is worse.

7. Individual responsibility is man's only moral and personal salvation. This responsibility is best realized through respect for and love for one's own soil.

8. There can be no salvation without suffering, and without a redeeming love that is a part of one's own consciousness. Man must become his God.

Where Faulkner's literature is not romantic naturalism, and not a near miss on Freudian levels, there are existential qualities. He does not reach the point where he prefers committing the self as self, without an object.

NORMAN MAILER

Mailer (1923–   ) has written *The Naked and the Dead* (1948), *Barbary Shore* (1951), *Deer Park* (1955), *Presidential Papers* (1960), and a few articles as his main contributions to literature. *The Naked and the Dead* (1948) has a World War II South Pacific island for its setting. The task is to defeat the Japanese. Within the structure of the novel, we have two times. One looks ahead in carrying out the war; the other, like Faulkner's time, stands still in terms of a past that reveals the consciousness of different kinds of individuals. The qualities of naturalism are evident: depraved people, a hostile environment, foul language, foul minds, foul characters, racism, minority protests, antiwar sentiment, and primitive actions, thoughts, and instincts. The qualities of existentialism are commitment, agony, despair, and possession. Cummings, whatever he may be politically, has the violent ruthlessness of an American, and the powerful intelligence of the French middle-class intellectualist. He completely stands to his own commitment and possesses, for his own freedom, Hearn. Hearn, a moral man who does not really know whether he is coming or going, represents a weak excursion into democracy. The young officer is completely dominated by the General Cummings. He enlists, but changes his mind at the last moment—too late. He can not commit himself to anything in terms of his own consciousness. He is an excellent example of Sartre's "bad faith" individual.

On the "lower" level, we have the Sergeant Croft and a private Valsen, but the parallel is not able to hold. Croft finally backs out. His commitment to the climbing of the mountain does not bring him to the fact of death, and he lies terribly to himself; worse, he is in complete bad faith because he could have gone on up the mountain and should have committed himself, but he let himself believe that he was what he was not—solicitous for the men, as they fled.

Valsen did not stand up to Croft at the critical moment; he did not commit himself to any facet within his own consciousness. If he had surrendered, on his own terms and on no one else's, there would have been the existential decision. He makes his decision against an external standard—authority. Mailer preferred his protests against external institutions, such as social injustice and war, to the existential concentration on selfhood. Goldstein, who measures up well in opposing the artistic soul to war and who endures and endures, can be placed only in a modern tragedy setting. The outside forces are great, but one suffers and endures, but only with the past beating against him. He is a dead person whom death never claims. When the decision has to be made, Mailer falls back on naturalism, with its ironies. Cummings' intellect and ruthlessness do not win the battle—that is won when he is not on the scene. Nature plays the ironic role, and is tabbed as the villain of the piece.

Barbary Shore (1951) shows us a fractured world, a world disintegrating when the bonds of personality snap, and when ideologies are tailored from the demands of individuals. To some degree, the individuals are tailored to the ideologies. McLeod presents, superficially, excellent existential credentials. As a communist, he has committed the beautiful crime lauded by Genet—betrayal of one's cause. Then he betrays the United States. He has taken the hope of the world with him. Hollingsworth is apparently a secret agent and a thorough servant of the state: he has the role of trying to recover the hope of the world from McLeod. He has powerful claims to existentialism. He is sadistic for its own pleasure, and in his own right. His world is himself in a self-consciousness that is pure hate. Other characters include the mad Lannie who is masochistic and anti-McLeod. Then there is the leftist Lannie, who, through possessing McLeod, regains his own identity and escapes with the hope of the world.

Mailer uses these people, together with two more, to develop his unconvincing points of view. The landlady, Guinevere, is anything except a Guinevere. Her huge bulk is symbolic of the unenlightened and sensual American masses. The child Monina, is the daughter of the landlady, and represents the coming world of people who will not dare to attempt reality. What could have turned to existentialism broke down into a horrible expression of naturalism. The people strike out with blind emotion and frightening violence against a world they cannot understand. Instead of finding that the consciousness of Hollingsworth is one that stands for himself and to himself, we find that he, also, hates, not as hating, but as hating the outside and political forces. "Hating" is existentialistic; "hating something" is essentialistic. The figures try to create a world of consciousness to match the irrational forces that press upon them. They stand committed to striking back at that thing called "life." In the light of what we know existential freedom to mean, we can not find its pure state here. Mailer allowed his anger at the capitalistic institution to permit the artistic mistake of forcing his characters to speak for himself. Given the opportunity for having a real expression of selfhood, he marred a potentially great artistic creation by resting on his own hazy, furry, and unsophisticated political ideologies. One is not an existentialist, if he is any other "ist." McLeod is a near miss in this novel, insofar as the existential mind is concerned. Given the opportunity to stand out through continued betrayals, he flubs the final test.

Deer Park (1955), or "Desert of Gold," has a Hollywood resort setting, but attempts universal symbolism. Mailer moves away from the traditional setting of naturalism as geographic and as class-structured so as to present the economically deprived. There is naturalism enough in the gold-domed Hollywood, but a naturalism of the spirit. Both Sergius and Eitel open the book in complete bad faith: Eitel has been slipping steadily and will not be honest with himself; he desires to make himself, as director, the rationalization for a poor writer, and contrariwise. Sergius is there only as a lucky man in a moment of gambling benignity; he is the narrator of the play and a devotedly committed person to one principle that he must never violate: never to commit himself. His consciousness is a seething maelstrom of crosscurrents, all adding up to indecision. His problem is not one of passivity, but of a nature that has a thousand impulses, all at cross purposes to each. Eitel is an example of a person who has lost his good faith in himself, turned to bad faith, and cannot find his way back. He comes closest to regeneration when he stands against an investigating committee in Congress.

Mailer's *Presidential Papers of Norman Mailer* (1960) consists of varied thoughts on and of the American scene. When Mailer stays out of politics, his art prospers. His best sections are those which reveal a keen spontaneous insight into experience. The papers reveal three main facets of his character: his ideology is leftist; he is strongly tinged with the color of naturalism; his selfhood often approaches the existential position. These positions are not always complementary. In his statement against capital punishment, his argument that the states that keep the capital punishment shall have a personal and bloody spectacle is unique. He combines his naturalism and his existential bent in the suggestion that, first, the killer would bear the guilt of his victim. The killer would also bear the guilt of having killed his victim. Finally, the killer would also bear the fact of his own death, as killer, to all people. Mailer believes that the American would like to see the gladiator back. Sadism would then be released. In Mailer's third paper, "The Existential Hero," Mailer refers to himself. He has a feeling of guilt and betrayal, but he has to stand behind his betrayal, and he has to stand so in public judgment. He believed that he had to stand and point to the direction and position in which he had placed the newly-elected President. He had to assume the responsibility, not for good, but for the negative aspects of his own influence on the readers. Although he believed that he was betraying the left, he had to accept the "hero's" role as guilt, his own guilt.

In his essay "The Existential Heroine," Mailer continued his concern with isolation, anxiety, relating his remarks to Mrs. Jacqueline Kennedy. Mailer's concern for the entire panorama that is the United States is his strongest point. That there is a political and panoramic existentialism we had not envisioned. But that in unity there is a desperate alienation is both probable and agonizing.

JACK KEROUAC

Kerouac (1922–   ) is one of the contemporary writers who is considered a member of the group known as the "beats." That he is a primitive romanticist is more than evident, and for originality of ideas he has little to offer. He comes closest to the existential mind in his emphasis on acting and on all other "ings," with little concept or relish for the object or purpose of the expressing. Basically, one can not be a pure existentialist unless he has an exceedingly powerful intellect, one capable of considerable abstraction, and one strong enough to bear considerable philosophic weight. Kerouac, then, has limitations in two areas. First, his jargon limits the number of potential readers to an age group between 18–25 or so. His speech utterances and patterns do not appeal to many readers within that age group. Second, his discussions boil down to movements, social disorganization, and other sociological problems. He might have learned his lesson from Upton Sinclair who discovered that pure food laws are considered more essential by the public than is pure air for the workers. Complaints, however humorous, about society's mores make for good sermons and good politics, but poor literature. However, a certain ruggedness of self is underneath an unfortunate idiom.

Kerouac's books appeal to college juniors and to beginning college instructors, and perhaps to teachers of urban high schools. There is a lively but humorous reaction against dead mores and traditions. There is a call to a permanent and habitual spring fever. At its least harmless, man takes to the road; at its worst there is a dangerously primitive amorality. Kerouac has positive features. He has been quick to grasp the high school and college dropout's problem—a complete isolation and alienation from traditional criteria which operate in a compelling and demanding fashion, one not meaningful or comprehensible to a sensitive but limited intellect.

When Kerouac is at such a point, his work is promising and rewarding; when we strip away the jargon and find a dislike of monotonous city life, with its degrading and depressing atmosphere, we are reminded of "Sociology 362." Attacks on the quality of the writing as style are somewhat unfortunate because the consciousness of the people he uses in his books corresponds well to his impressionistic and highly nervous idiom. If his people do not form plots about life, he would be dishonest were he to do so. We must avow that he is true to his materials. Whether we like his stuff of life or not, such stuff does exist, and should be a matter of literary attention and notice.

BERNARD MALAMUD

Malamud (1914–   ) a talented writer, has left the provincial Jewish ghetto to step into the wider and more universal minority picture. He cannot leave alone the experience of those deprived and dispossessed, but falls back on the myths of the Jewish past. Given a personality primarily Hellenic—an exquisite lyrical range, a bent toward the aesthetic ideal of the Greek—he cannot remain away from the deadening grasp of Hebraism. If there is no gloom, he will darken the universe with allegory; if there is no injustice, he will limit his horizon to a place where injustice can and must be found. When there is no one to lead out of slavery, he will create his own fierce agony. When he has wrung the last drops of pity and despair from himself and the reader, he will turn to a thoroughgoing mysticism.

Malamud's most positive virtue, among many, is his ability to avoid being a middle-class Philistine, although he can moralize with the best of them. He has some of the Gothic qualities of Faulkner, thus ensuring that American writing will continue its anti-Hellenic bent. When we move to his specific positions, we find that the world is absurd because man must fail. Whatever he knows is not enough for this universe. Because this universe does not furnish a reality to equate with man's knowledge, he seeks a reality that does. But he cannot get out of this world. Because he belongs to those who have always had to accommodate and to adjust to the irrationality of people in this world and to this world, accommodation is a natural response. Such a "stay here" demands courage, or at least some rugged endurance.

To insist that man's own knowledge, as reality, is that of the world of Nature is to shatter one's self through trying to impose myth on a derisive Nature. That electron which is the basic particle of matter and the stuff of the mind, ironically, misleads man as to the truth of his own reality.

Malamud has much to do with bird symbolism and with saints, but his saints are not the loftiest of all possibilities: they are taken from those who are essentially mystical but earthbound, like St. Francis. Malamud is too honest to step away from the fact of materialism, and he is existentialistic. In considering his qualities we find that:

1. His saints never remain aloft very long; nor are they incalculably remote from experience.

2. Man must accept the fact that he is under moral necessities and pressures: we mean that Malamud insists that a man must always say to himself what "ought" to be done. Like the Moses of old and the pioneer of the West, he will not go very far before he will raise a temple of duty between himself and the sun.

3. His duty is deterministic, almost one with the force and impact of the Calvinistic demand that one impale himself upon the cross of "must." One does not willingly elect to be moral; he must acknowledge "must."

4. His heroes know what they should be, but because they also know what they are, bad faith is the central existential fact for Malamud. The pessimism that permeates his art is revealed in the fact that his characters do not all go to the new position, or, if they are there, they lack the staying power.

5. Malamud uses the epic strain in developing his local hero, but the reader is too sophisticated to buy the descendant, even when the myth is used in a perverted sense. The reader knows that we have no possibility of finding any kind of a Helen of Troy or Cleopatra. If Malamud were to consider an Aneas-like figure rejecting Dido, the modern Aneas and Dido would not be either continual or continuous with history. If they are not so, Malamud cannot show why they are not.

6. Malamud's heroes always have a price, and the selling point is reached when the hero's ability and the standard the universe requires clash, with the hero losing out.

7. Suffering is the least that man can settle for; at the very least, he must meet the fact that he and the environment are not equal.

8. Suffering means committing the self to action; the result of committing one's self to engaging life is suffering.

9. The higher the flight, the more the suffering. Because man cannot find a reality in himself sufficient for experience, his agony over the terrible differential is his success.

10. Love involves both acceptance and rejection of the "other." Consciousness of a fellow being in a common experience is at the heart of love, and love is its heart.

11. Experience involves engagement; engagement results in suffering through seeing the determinism in a life that shows man and his fatal flaw, not enough knowledge, or the wrong kind of knowledge. Through suffering with the insight that one's fellow mortal is enduring the same lot, comes love.

12. Love is not freely bestowed on man.

13. Malamud uses archetypes (the original pattern of forms; things are only copies) to give his works more universal significance: Achilles sulking in his tent; Aeneas casting away Dido; and St. Francis feeding the birds.

14. A quality of his work is the attempt of the individual to commit himself to himself, admitting that his freedom is but a matter of degree.

RALPH ELLISON

On a universal level a man identifies his life with his self, with his self as determined by the outside, with the outside determined by the self. And, if he is dead or insane, nothing is determined by anything, insofar as the specific Joe Jones is concerned, except the "other" who is conscious of him. When one belongs to a group that is characterized by "others" so that such characterization sets up a standard which is reflected in qualities or characteristics of the individuals in the group, a situation that could be abstract becomes real, concrete.

During the past sixty years Americans have seen the German in the light of sociological, philosophical, and ideological statements made about him. Some of the statements have been made by the Germans, some of the statements by others. Our consciousness of the German has been determined by our own condition as reflected in our own economic, sociological, political, and philosophical natures. As well, we have had direct contact with Germans. Our attitudes are brought into play—whereas, in such provinces as geometry and horticulture, our beliefs are brought into play. We can make the same statement about Fascism, Communism, Pan-Israelism, or Pan-Africanism. Apart from our consciousness concerning the physical world and its laws, we have the various kinds of consciousness that involve us intimately, and emotionally.

We need not go that far afield; we can consider country and city, suburbia and slums, Yankee and Southerner. Whenever people are different through dialect, political affiliation, religious affiliation, educational philosophy, and the old school tie, consciousness within the contexts we indicate as consciousness is modified in the light of its emotive states. The structure of consciousness itself may become so rigid as to prevent consciousness flowing. By "flowing," we mean engaging itself with suppleness toward experience. There will be, in a supple consciousness, an engagement with experience and a willingness to enter a wide range of situations.

In the terrible dissonance of dissent characterized by extreme movements we see the sad verification of our observations: "leftist versus rightist," "nationalism versus internationalism," "Negro versus white," "employer versus employee," "John Birch Society versus Communism," and "NAACP versus the Ku Klux Klan."

What happens when the individual belongs to a minority group whose members are bound by a rigid code imposed by a majority group that has the power to enforce its views? What happens to the American Negro? We shall look at his condition from his side. We not only see Negro*ness* in the other; but we impose what we see. We do not see the individual Negro,

but we see that image we call Negro*ness* and the image is not
the Negro, but the Negro in the context of what we have determined him to be. We have given him the qualities of myth
and symbol. He furnishes only the visual concretization of the
symbol or myth within whose framework, as reality, physically, he happens to stand.

With our pervasive stereotyping, we can see why Jewish-
American writers and our Negro writers should turn toward
existential thinking and feeling. The Negro not only lives in a
wider community that has determined to treat him as within
the context of predetermined codes and standards, but the individual Negro lives in his own community of Negroes, and that
community has its own symbol and myth for dealing with the
majority group. Where does the individual Negro stand? He is
an individual within a country, of which he is a citizen, that
has attitudes toward peoples and their ideologies in other countries. He is a part of a country that has symbols and myths
concerning him, and which symbols and myths are held in
such strength as to compel his attention physically, intellectually, and spiritually. He lives within his own community,
which has its symbols and myths as to how he must react toward other Negroes, toward the majority group, and toward
his country's view on the worldwide panorama. He has a
frightening world to which he must attend. What must he accommodate to? What shall be the basic structure of his consciousness?

Whatever he does, there is one basic fact. He does not change
his color, except by intermarriage, and then only possibly in his
children. But the individual does not even do that; he can do
that only for the other—his descendants. We are concerned
with the individual Negro who is his color. There is no question about the psychological aspects of the unique in the per-

ceptual world. What is unusual? What is rare? What are unusual and rare that strike our attention? A gold ball among white ones; a red dress when all others are white; a poodle in the midst of St. Bernards—all these are perceived uniquely. Apart from physical stimuli, there are the intellectual, spiritual, and emotive aspects reflected by the outside community and by the individuals within the unique group. To a person who is black, his perceptions of himself as black, and of others as of some other color, must differ.

While he needs the same food, religion, philosophy, psychology, economics, and satisfaction of basic drives as does any other person, he does not "need" to change his color. If the pressures were great enough, and great enough to make a difference between living and dying, he would change his color if he could, as would a small group of white people in a vast Negro society. Or he would change his attitude if such a change would be sufficient for survival. A Jewish person can change his name; a German can change his name; an Irishman can change his name, if changing his name will bring about acceptance of him, and if he needs such acceptance. But a Japanese, an Indian, or a Negro will not gain the same advantage or disadvantage by changing his name, for he retains the color which distinguishes him. What a Negro must do, or what the majority must do, is to change the myth or symbol binding the consciousness of the individuals within the group. Against such a framework, and within such a framework, Negro writers express themselves. The Negro writer writes about life, and such life is white and red as well as black. To that extent he is a Negro but not a Negro, but a writer. As a Negro whose consciousness is determined by the immediacy of everyday experience, he is a Negro in a white world.

Ralph Ellison is a Negro writer. We shall consider him primarily in the context of his existential qualities. The *Invisible Man* reveals the number of identifications that must take place within the consciousness of the Negro. As the Mason passes through his rites and rituals on his Masonic pilgrimage, so the Negro goes through successive modifications of his consciousness, each taking on ritualistic force. The story starts in the South, from where the Negro must always start spiritually, if not physically. The hero Lucius receives some good existential advice from his dying grandfather. The Negro community can keep its identity, and the Negro within the group must keep his own identity. He must be certain that he is completely possessed by the Southern community. The Negro can "bloat" the Southerners, forcing himself on Southern consciousness, and, once in a while, on the Southern conscience.

The boy tried to please the people in the community, the white people. He made a speech at his graduation and was considered the best-educated Negro in the town. To keep him from having any respect for himself, he was put in a battle royal the next night against other Negroes, and betrayed into fighting the toughest of them all. He was beaten and then humiliated when he delivered his graduation address to the white people. He was nearly beaten when he used the words "social responsibility." On the inside of the briefcase he was given for his speech were these words: "Keep this nigger running." He did not understand their meaning then.

JAMES BALDWIN

Baldwin (1924–   ) is a militant American-Negro writer who takes his problems of identity angrily, and lashes out, often blindly, at forces that frustrate him. These forces are the same forces that make life for a deprived minority a miserable experience. When one is also dispossessed, his frustration and fury are equally augmented. However little a person has to be dispossessed from, he needs that little. A Negro writer, or any other Negro, who needs to create his own identity or who needs to find his own identity has to fight against his own community of Negroes, and against the major community—major in size and influence. His own community will reject him if he desires to assimilate and to accommodate to the white community when such accommodation is different from the relationships permitted by the Negro community.

Baldwin, like any other figure—Negro, Indian, Chinese, or Caucasian—seeks identity at the risk of rejection. Now, a tragic figure traditionally welcomes such rejection. He spurns his communities and stands happy in his alienation. When any person demands that he be accepted, and when his demands are "demanding" in the full sense of the word, he encounters problems. Because he is an artist, a writer, he runs into the full gamut of opposition encountered by the artist who arbitrarily fastens on all experience for his devouring imagination. For the artist who is Negro, and for the reader who is Negro or anything else, there is the added problem that the artist does not know whether his despair and fury come from frustration as an artist or as a Negro. The reader has to suspend his judgments in the field of art and in the field of sociological experience. The reader cannot be ignorant of the attitudes of men toward their fellow men in day-by-day images of individuals and the groups they are in. Therefore, if Baldwin has been "hammered" by the critics, some of his resentment is justified; but much is not.

Where art and propaganda begin and end and where they should begin and end in the same piece of work are not easy matters to resolve. A cry of protest at a specific situation is still art unless the writer prefers his protest to his art. Baldwin has been unjustly treated in this province: his work is art, and, if his art is uneven, he is living in a very uneven age.

Baldwin is not content to state, but he states so that his assertions have the force of religious commandments: many times this emphasis on "oughts" arouses sharp adverse reaction from reader and critic. But the existential elements are clearly present in Baldwin's writing. We are not always clear about the purpose for which Baldwin's heroes seek to establish a thwarted identity, but the very lack of clarity indicates on Baldwin's part a basic honesty. His heroes are not allowed to enter the worlds of experience. But which worlds? Are they prevented as artists, as the Negro who seeks the larger community of all mankind, as the Negro who wishes to enter the Negro world, as the Negro who wishes to create a world of whites and blacks, or as a Negro who wants to enter the white world? Perhaps every one to some degree, and no one world to every degree.

He is attacked for his themes of homosexuality, sensuality, violence, and profanity; these elements are present in his art, and they are often unpleasant. But that they destroy the artistic integrity of his art is not established. The lack of their presence would be questionable. There are two solid objections to his use of abnormal forms of behavior: one is that he writes in such a manner to commercialize his art. Whether true or not, the accusation cannot be proven. The other is that he is stating a case for naturalism. If he is so stating, then his case for identity as being thwarted by social conditions is not as convincing, for in naturalism, everyone is thwarted. In fact, the one who is most happy with his identity either accepts a completely determined universe, or he rebels on the same basis as anyone who finds living up to a concept of "free will" difficult.

SAUL BELLOW

Bellow (1915–   ) is another brilliant novelist in the tradition of Jewish-American writers. Using the word "tradition" seems ironical when these writers are wrestling with a world whose traditions are shattered and whose traditions they have helped to shatter. But we say tradition because Bellow, Malamud, Gold, Goldman, Roth, among other such writers, are our dominant and most literate spokesmen in contemporary literature. They have established a tradition among themselves, and reading one is often very much like reading another. What the French intellectuals have done in France, and Britain's angry men (and not so very angry men) have done in the British Isles, these writers are doing in the United States. Ironically, they are well respected at home in the United States, but considered not as universal in scope as England's young writers and France's contemporary set. There must be something about the United States with its rich variety of landscape and types that makes our writers quite provincial; a monstrous but observable irony.

Bellow, like Nietzsche in his art expression, has been lucky. The ground has been broken for him and his path made easier. What he might have fought for earlier, escape from the cruel America ghetto, has been substantially achieved; therefore, he is freed for attacks on the entire American ghetto. We might well pause to indicate the basic qualities we expect to find in the writing of Bellow and his contemporaries, even his predecessors.

1. We have the remaining traces of the American-Jewish writer who had to fight American prejudice, naturalism, and their leftist leanings during the depression—among these we had West and Henry Roth.

2. We have the traces of Bellow's contemporaries who oppose war, authoritarianism, persecution, and intellectual sterility.

3. We have the liberal Jewish-American writer whose brilliant imagination was entangled with ideologies primarily socialist and leftist, and who, because of such intermingling, encountered not personal maltreatment, but rejection in an America turning away from the leftism of the 1930's. Such writers as Trilling and Schwartz were disillusioned with the promises of the left.

Bellow inherits and accompanies these diverse trends. Out of his plasma comes a heritage of alienation, isolation, solitude, suffering, endurance, cynicism, and even plodding perseverance. But today, Bellow and his fellow Jewish-American writers must write "what they are." They are citizens of the United States and what is American is their perceptual consciousness at the very least. The American scene is the scene for and of their writing. What they have to accommodate to is this scene in all of its middle-class aspects. For many dreary years, Bellow's predecessors were anxious to obtain a slice of the middle-class life; they have the slice, and they now know what their fellow Americans have known for a long time: the taste is bitter, arid, and sterile. Fitzgerald and Sinclair Lewis could do nothing with American life of the lower middle class, the middle middle class, and the upper middle class and the upper class. Bellow has found out that enforced physical alienation perhaps is better than spiritual alienation, but he has to keep what his predecessors have bought so dearly.

The cost has yet to be paid, not in Bellow's lifetime, for there is no possibility that any man will be German and American at the same time or Jewish and American at the same time or Polish and American at the same time. The only identity that can be maintained, if the Negro cares to maintain his identity, is that of the Negro—because he stands out by virtue of color. So Bellow's choice, as the main choice, is that of every American: how to keep one's identity in this kind of a world. He adds to his problems by harassing himself about the left, and by forcibly maintaining a ghetto in his own mind. His view of alienation is but a plaything compared to Sartre's and Genet's real thing. The reader is cautioned that Bellow suffers easily: he has a background of suffering, but his is raised to an art that is almost artificial, in the way that frosting can be laid on the cake so as not to seem an integral part of its ingredients. Bellow decided to be a "highbrow" in literature. There was too much competition from Salinger on the commuter's level. Bellow as Jewish is like Malamud, Wouk, and Salinger in many respects, one of them being that he dare not get too far away from Jewish material. His Jewish heroes are intellectual, but he does not make them heroic. Nor does he have them in physical flight. They do not like the brutal depersonalization of war, but they are not unsoldierly, nor are they defiant of the military. Bellow's stature is indicated in that his characters behave credibly, as characters must behave when they are waiting, waiting, and waiting.

Bellow writes about anti-semitism as any other intelligent Jewish writer writes about that prejudice. He reaches the truth because his mind has the ability to take the specific theme or situation and reach a significant point. He must use Jewish characters in part because he must stay with his real material. But the product of the artistic experience is an aesthetic object, not Jewish, not American, not Anglo-Saxon, and not any slice of race, religion, or nationality. The answer, for Bellow, is that when man reacts with another man, and does so with any ideology, prejudice, and bias in mind or heart, each destroys the other. One cannot be destroyed without also being the destroyer. We are at the existential position of possessing, creating, having, and existing. If a man exists as something other than the self, he will be annihilated as an annihilator. If a man who, as A, engages with hate in himself for another person B, who is conscious of that hate, A and B will destroy each other.

WIRT WILLIAMS

The works of Williams (1921–   ) have suffered the fate that can befall a writer who can be placed in the category of naturalism, romantic revolt against regimentation, modern Gothic restatement of Faulkner's thesis concerning Southern culture, a popularity-seeker on best-seller lists, and a neoexpressionist of modern idiomatic expressions, sexual sadism, and the sterility of human beings. Williams is nearly an existentialist, for he has strong existential qualities. We must view Williams as a writer who indicates that the existential point of view comes through, but its proponents make no more of their commitment in death than they do in life. Williams takes his characters away from institutions to show them how they behave when they have no external moral and ethical codes binding them. From Williams the reader can obtain the spiritual alienation of his Southerners who are aeons away from the old code of the gentleman. As Faulkner pointed out, the code was to be alienated from the entire code. Particularly depressing are the male members of New Orleans and the rest of his Louisiana society. The women are much stronger as human beings, equally amoral and immoral, for Williams has the rare gift of drawing feminine characters well.

J. D. SALINGER

The literature of Salinger (1919–   ) arouses little controversy; therefore, this significant writer is being evaluated more fairly than those mentioned earlier. The proper evaluation must come from somewhere in the hazy bounds of different critical positions. A careful reading of his books is the best answer to any difficulty in understanding his position. Holden Caulfield, Salinger's *Catcher in the Rye* "hero," will serve as a central focus for discussing the author.

Salinger is astute enough to know that one does not banish, in a genii-like fashion, the evidence of mind, spirit, and body. In cultured society a sophisticated person might be able, at will, to induce a psychological field strong enough to obliterate all consciousness of the world and all of man but the irrational feeling of self. Such an individual is not Holden Caulfield, and such a culture is not American. By an activity forcefully directed at negating the world of absolutes, Salinger and his "heroes" destroy outside reality. By profanity, by vulgarity, and by iconoclasm, Holden makes the outside world of church, school, and other social institutions microscopic. Having done so, he can then wash his hands of any responsibility to them. As habitual drinking can induce drunken states, his repetition of words in themselves of a belittling nature can belittle the world. Holden uses the self to express the world as "phony"; in a reflection of the terms Holden uses, his viewing self sees the world as the words have designated the world. Salinger will not banish the world of institutions materially; such a world is needed for heroes like Holden.

A critic, Bowen, observes that Salinger militates against traditional structures, and that our youths, because they are rebels, adopt the Salinger point of view. He considers that naturalistic details reduce the traditional ideal vision and that the incessant cursing orients the reader toward a nonvertical view of the universe. Holden's comments on Christianity, on Jesus, on Benedict Arnold, or on any thesis representing good or evil figures in a traditional sense, are deflating and profanely so. Holden revolts against traditional institutions—not because they are always bad, but because he sometimes does not understand them. Holden objects to the grim world of naturalism, for he is not the stuff of which heroes are made. He rejects the world of ideas and emotions because he must be drawn outward toward them. All that he cannot fit within his experience as revealing to himself, and to no one else, as an acceptable picture of himself, must be obliterated.

Salinger is on stronger ground than the reader might think at first glance. The American temperament is strongly materialistic, and the rational force in American life has gone to support a material world. In slashing away at the material world of man, Salinger attacks not only the material world, but also its support—reason. When Holden calls his old history teacher a "phony," Holden means that the old teacher, who tried to help him, stands as a force that intrudes itself between Holden and a positive apprehension of himself. Had the teacher made such impacts on Holden as to serve only for a mirror to Holden's views of himself as "feeling" significant, the teacher would not be a "phony." When the outside world reduces itself to destroying in order to create Holden as a living apprehension to himself, the world of experience is not phony, of course. The reader must understand that any experience that would make Holden call a person or idea "good" for itself would be disastrous. Salinger's characters must experience living so that all of the world of experience is covered by each individual's experience, if only of his own living. One way to avoid setting up outside experience is to ensure that no terms or thoughts are ever applied to such experience, other than in a derogatory sense.

Holden tells us that he has no wind, that he is a pacifist, that he was happy because he nearly cried, "if you want to know the truth." "You" refers to the world, the phony world. If the world values good physical condition, then Holden has no wind. If the world values fighting for country, then Holden is a "pacifist." "Happy" and "bawling"—for "crying"—are absolutes, absolutes that society can assimilate as symbols that have a wide range of acceptance. Holden negates them for the world.

As to the story itself, there is a myth, and the myth is a parallel of Mark Twain's Huckleberry Finn. Holden wants to know who he is, to find his identity, but he never succeeds, other than in actualizing all futures into a sustained present as *non compos mentis.* Huckleberry Finn came as close to finding himself as Holden did not, and retained his sanity. Huck may never get all the way there, but he will not finish the trip in a strait jacket: he will also be, at any time, a better existentialist than poor Holden. From a point of view a competent critic should not reject, the book has a central problem in the area of art: Holden cannot stand out against a world he does not understand, unless the world is simply a symbol of his "standing out." But no such evidence appears as forceful. "Expressing" is one matter, and the adult consciousness of "possessing," "having," "creating," and "existing" are other problems. To "reject" implies a human position whereby one has been "there" and has understood what he objects to. Holden is not without keen perception, but he has not reached the point where his view of the world as "phony" carries any more weight than the word "damn" when there is no more damnation.

Holden's existential leanings are marked, particularly his assumption of guilt and pain for all the others. So completely does he possess the rest of the world that we expect to see him enthroned in a vast void.

HERBERT GOLD

Gold (1924–   ) is in the existential tradition, and is one of America's finest novelists over the past decade and a half. However, a very solid criticism can and should be levied against him; the same one brought against Salinger, Malamud, and Bellow, among others. There is far too much lack of spontaneity of consciousness among his characters. They are not given enough Hellenism to make their human predicament meaningful. The characters are drab, for the most part. The reader almost begs that the great annihilator should take them mercifully away. We regret that Gold does not know better people in his novels than he does know, but considering their low potential, he goes as far as he can go, honestly, with them.

His principal novels are *Birth of a Hero* (1951), *The Prospect Before Us* (1954), *The Man Who Was Not With It* (1956), *The Optimist* (1959), *Therefore, Be Bold,* (1960), and *Salt* (1963). When we consider the titles, we must make two conclusions as to possibility: optimism or irony. The characters are forward-looking—or they are just the opposite. The criticism is frequently made that Gold's characters are not sufficiently put into the fire, as compared to and with those of the more vigorous existentialists—Malraux and Sartre, for example. His opening novel is not his best, and the firecracker of a man is not of heroic stuff. We have to accept the fact that our American existentialists, with the exception of Williams in *Ada Dallas* and *A Passage of Hawks,* serve up fairly weak sinners

—and, in all, Williams is not entirely an existentialist, except in his novel *A Passage of Hawks*.

Gold is always looking for some accommodation. The poetry of profanity and sex are handled in the usual competent way found in American-Jewish writing. There must be enough suffering, yet enough endurance to weld experience into the poetry that can come only when the personality, as reduced as its scope may be, has the elements of the heart, mind, and body. In this Judaic-Christian concept of man as one who can evolve from voidness to fullness, we have the difference between Sartre and Gold. Bud Williams' confession is in reality a commitment to accommodate to the world. The protagonist and his wife make the inevitable "Goldian" adjustment or accommodation to this world of reality as physical and human. They are not a delightful pair. We have narcotics, adolescent passion, and a paternal-filial battle; we know enough about the existential—and the naturalistic—mind to know that each of three problems involves destructive possessions and the mutual devouring of each other's self. The smaller the carnival and the smaller its people, the more vicious, depraved, and nauseating its character. Finally, when a human being is reduced to his foulest levels, we cannot accept mankind so near the purely primitive level without a revolt. From that revolt comes passionate pity.

WILLIAM GOLDMAN

Goldman (1931–   ) attempts to combine naturalism and existentialism. He wrote his first novel in 1957 (*Temple of Gold*). He then followed with *Soldier in the Rain* (1960) and *Boys and Girls Together* (1964). *Temple of Gold* has naturalism as method and existentialism as thought. The sheer weight of facts and human society make intellectual involvement difficult, at the best, and disastrous, at the worst: and Goldman makes such statements through his characters.

Boys and Girls Together (1964), like *Temple of Gold* and *Soldier in the Rain,* washes quite a bit of rough material from the characters. Goldman, with all of his dazzling metaphor, could listen to Frost with profit, and leave a little hidden dirt on the human potato—the natural state of each. This book is over six hundred pages long, and, from a technical point of view, is characterized by little descriptive detail, little psychoanalysis, but much dialogue and many situations. Goldman has furnished the raw immediacy of experience for his characters, but much of the experience is of the same type. That statement is no condemnation, for we can see that his characters, for all of their mobility, are capable of a limited range of experience. He has exploited that limit for all of its worth.

Existentialism and naturalism can take a short walk together, but they have to separate when the author claims that present choice is determined by all past neural experiences, many of them driven well below conscious level. The existential writer expects the character to find his identity in the present immediacy of experience. Goldman's main problem with his sets of deviant and seamy characters is not with their utter repulsiveness, but with trying to validate existentialism through the grimmest and most uncompromising naturalism.

JOHN UPDIKE

Updike (1932–   ) has the qualities of subtlety, precision, clarity, unorthodoxy, insight, and individuality. *The Poorhouse Fair* (1959) strikes a blow for commitment, but to utopias. Here there is a commitment to self, to consciousness of the self as free, if only for one actualization of time.

In *Rabbit, Run* (1960), Updike is an angry man when he sees man choosing poorly and being poorly chosen. There is not much that is admirable in Rabbit, but Updike does not let that little drain away.

EDWARD ALBEE

Albee (1928–   ) is not an individualist, although he starts with the individual's inability to escape his alienation, his isolation, and his despair at not being able to reconcile his uniqueness with that of the group. He longs to be at one with his fellow man, but to be so is to face the fact of his own failures—because man is a social animal. No communication at all is disastrous; communication is equally so. In the *Zoo Story,* produced in Berlin in 1959, the curse is not loneliness, but being "lonely." In the United States, grim naturalism, as expressed through the brutal language of Steinbeck and Hemingway, as well as through the violent language of Miller and O'Neill, emphasized a need for group dynamics. Man must adopt a code to oppose the depersonalizing force of nature, to escape being identified with the continuously whirling and apparent purposeless stirring of the atoms and molecules.

Now we find that naturalism is rejected because, in a group situation, man has doubly accentuated his problem. In addition to being hammered at by the concept of a limitless universe, but of a limited "him," comprehensible only through submicroscopic particles, he is now battered by the pressures of his fellow men. They impose their sterility on him, or he projects his into them. If he remains with the group, he sees either their sterility or he sees his own in them, with the members acting as a mirror. Thus, he becomes existential. Cutting himself away from the group, he is now his own mirror. But he cannot escape his predicament. There is a truth within him, one that can not be stilled forever. He can have no meaning for anyone, nor for himself, apart from Bill, Joe, and Sue.

The Sandbox is an assault on the isolation of American families from real communication. The people use no given names and include The Young Man, Mommy, Daddy, Grandma, The Musician. The mother and father enact the role of being on the beach; in saying the beach is cold, the father is thinking of the outside world; the wife assures him that she is warm; she is referring to their inside world of customs and acquaintanceship. The young man represents the angel of death. When they wave and he waves back, they are merely going through mechanical operations. In their next conversation we find the grandmother (eighty-six) is going to die; the father moves to alienate her since she is not his mother, but his wife's.

Who's Afraid of Virginia Woolf? takes into account the stream-of-consciousness technique, the wolf as an animal and symbol, and introduces a further irony in contrasting the meaningful material that flowers through Virginia Woolf's consciousness as contrasted with these distorted and malformed souls. Set in New England, in a small college town, there are four people: big but well-preserved Martha, fifty-two; thin, graying George, her younger husband, forty-six; Honey, twenty-six, blonde, no raving beauty; Nick, thirty, handsome. The mask is stripped from each individual who is left naked, ashamed, and, one might hope, purged. Whether the truth will set them free or not is a conundrum. At least the truth will show what one has to be free from. At the best, they will know what they have to be free *for*. Facing the truth is also complicated by the fact that forgiveness will be difficult. How does one forgive those he has wronged? Everyone in the play has wronged someone else. If the enemy is not a wolf, but an illusion of a wolf, then no one need be afraid. But there has been communication. If we look at the wolf as a symbol of evil, we still fear the wolf, but he is no longer in sheep's clothing. We know our own predicament, and we see the common enemy. At least we can communicate about that.

In each of the relationships, each individual has exercised bad faith and has refused to choose his own nature, positive or negative. Each reveals that he or she has given way to social accommodation. Each person fears facing life. The older woman, Martha, is disappointed that her husband, George, is not an important figure at the college where she is the daughter of the college president. She drinks; she is older than George, and she scorns his lack of industry. George can attack only her drinking and her years. Each has agreed on one point: they try to maintain the fiction of having a son. Nick reveals that his wife, Honey, took advantage of him in marrying him; we learn that he married her for her money. Each is engaged in trapping himself and the others into truth. George, wounded by his wife's attempted infidelity, crushes Martha by announcing that their son has been killed in an automobile accident: she can never keep up the fiction of a son again.

The play fails in one serious respect. There is no conviction that because one is brought face to face with the truth, even to the point of being honest with the self, he will choose to commit himself to choosing good faith for the self and with the self. Perhaps their alienation is from an essentialism they would like to enjoy, not as a result of an existentialism whose cruel facts would be too much reality to bear.

WILLIAM STYRON

Styron (1925–   ) uses a Faulknerian stream-of-consciousness technique frequently, and a unified seventeenth-century metaphysical personality in his writing. He has all the death, decay, and rot of the *Duchess of Malfi* and the tough intellect of Donne. His use of local themes, those of Virginia and farther South, should not keep the reader from pursuing universals.

Styron, like Malamud, uses a Jewish boy in his novels because the Jews have had long training in suffering and enduring. Harry had more than his share. Peyton married him, seeking a father more than a husband. Finally, he had had enough of her. Despair, anguish, and horror wracked her, as she saw that the joy she wanted and the pain she forced on everyone, as projected from herself, must be all hers. There is to be no salvation or damnation apart from herself. She stands alone. There is only one home to go to, but she must arise from the light in ashes, only after lying down in the dark. The light had already started for her when she made the plunge. For who can not say that the greatest agony of all is to forgive one's self and the greatest victory! If there is any single facet that should cause deep introspection from this novel, a good candidate for the honor should be the realization that whatever is intensely evil or good in the life of an individual comes from the consciousness of one's own, unique and aware self as responsible for its own destiny.

Glossary

ABSURDITY For the existentialist, the term is the condition perceived by the individual. Absurdity does not carry the meaning of being "ridiculous." When the existentialist finds that he has cut himself off from all traditional beliefs in past epical, ethical, and religious concepts of the nature of man, he has arrived at the point where he sees life without purpose, without design, and without hope. He then finds such a condition an "absurdity."

AGONY The condition in which the existentialist finds himself as a result of realizing that his decision to choose or his decision not to choose has bound others, as well as himself.

ALIENATION For the existentialist this is a state reached after the individual has paid a price. The price paid is that of actually choosing, willing, and deciding to be free from all external control that may come from institutions, events, laws, people, and ideas exterior and external to himself. If such a price is not paid, "alienation" or "isolation" is not attained and suffered. There is no alienation unless the price has been paid by an individual who makes the separation from society complete through his own continuous consciousness of rejecting all claims of man and nature. Thus, alienation is the state of liberation from all forces other than the choosing self, but is also the servitude forced on the individual who is conscious that he is rejecting a concept that must exist since he is always conscious of being forced to reject that concept continually.

ANGUISH The suffering process that accompanies each decision to choose, a decision which must place the existentialist outside of and/or in opposition to any externally-imposed standard.

ANTHROPOCENTRISM   The view that the world is primarily man-centered. This essentialistic view is not acceptable to the existentialist. He believes that the world is in terms of each individual who chooses and who makes his own world. The existentialist would say that he accepts "each man-centered world," if that world is entirely his own creation.

ATHEISM   This does not carry, for the existentialist, the ordinary denotative and connotative meanings held by the essentialist. The existentialist does not regard a god or God as an issue since he can as readily will or choose to bring into his own consciousness the existence of a god or God, as he can deny such existence.

ATTITUDE   This refers, psychologically, to a complex of beliefs and emotions. These beliefs and emotions, repeated in similar behavorial situations, result in specific attitudes—which, in turn, when added or fused, constitute the personality of the individual. Any attitude of the existentialist must be saturated with anxiety and anguish for each choice is a new experience, with no external criteria as guides.

BEING   A permanent experience as a process of each man's existence and of man's existence. Each gulping of experience from a future, which is conceded as an approaching death, results in choosing: the willing to choose carries a stream of conscious events, a stream which can properly be termed "becoming." Being is the beginning, middle, and end of the existing which has meaning to an individual only insofar as he wills, endures, decides, chooses, suffers, and agonizes.

BEING-IN-ITSELF   The condition of existence in action, devoid of any such terms as "could be," "may be," "should," "would," "possible," and "impossible." Such terms would imply existence as being conditioned by external standards which could control or modify "being." "Being-in-Itself" postulates an existence allowing individuals—and each individual—to engage in actions entirely within their own consciousness.

BEING-FOR-ITSELF   This term, defined in Sartrian terms, the only consistent existential terms, eliminates any dichotomy or split between the mind and the body. In this existential position, the mind is considered as the flow of experience which reveals the consciousness of self to the self. In Being-for-Itself there is no fusion or integration between body and the flow of consciousness —as mind. The two are one and the same. This position is mandatory for the existentialist. If he does not subsume body within his own consciousness as existing, he would find part of himself, as body, controlled by the external world of nature and man. Such a condition, for him, would be disastrous. His senses, as part of his body, would be enslaved to outside forces he calls the "others."

BELIEF   That form of knowledge which each individual holds as subject to proof by means available to like members of like societies: this belief is stated in essentialistic terms. The existential view of belief is the knowledge that a man must obtain from the flow of his own consciousness of emotional and intellectual components. This knowledge tells him that through choosing, willing, suffering, and agonizing, he has a unique insight into his own existence.

CERTAINTY   In the essentialistic view, certainty carries meanings of viewing sensory, intellectual, and emotive phenomena as predictable, verifiable, and reliable. "Certainty," to the existentialist, is an entirely relative experience. The only certainty he admits to is the inevitability that he is free, through choosing, to choose or not to choose, and through choosing, to act or not to act. Because each decision or choice will involve a new set of circumstances, no event, law, or standard can be "certain."

CHOICE   For the existentialist, this is the horror and glory, concurrently, of his existence. His freedom from the external world
demands that he must choose alternatives "blindly." The horror,
for him, is the anxiety and agony he experiences, for he knows
that he binds others as well as himself by his inevitable choosing,
or not choosing. He can, of course, choose not to choose.

CLASSICISM   That essentialistic literary philosophy which de-
fines all classics—and each classic—as those which involve thinking with feeling about things, ideas, events, institutions, and
people in the right proportion at the right time. The existentialist
might well approve the process implicit in this definition, but
would consider that no classic could exist apart from his own
consciousness and decision—which, even then, would be good
for only one time, place, and literary piece.

COMMUNION   That process which considers the senses, the
sense, and the sensibility (body, mind, and heart) as pleasurable
for their own beings, and as aesthetic in nature. The existentialist extends this self-consciousness to communing with his self.
The self is seen as a suffering, willing, choosing, alienated, and
agonizingly free spirit. Its joy is "three parts pain."

CONFLICT   That complex of decisions which involve opposition to being forced to conform to external standards, opposition
to being possessed by the thoughts and emotions of "others," and
opposition to being chosen by death and for death—his conflict
finds a continual series of choices, each of which results in his
decision to seek his own death.

COSMOCENTRISM   The thesis that one looks to the macroscopic
and external world of phenomena for the sources of mind, body,
and spirit. There is no question that this view is totally unacceptable to the existentialist who decries any form of naturalism.

CRISIS   A way of life for the existentialist. Crisis comes with each experience for there is always that moment when the decision to make a choice or not to make a choice brings agony, despair, anxiety, and the sense of alienation. The choice that binds the chooser as well as the chosen must always be accompanied by the despair of alienation because the choice is always made within by the individual who looks only within his own nature.

DADAISM   A movement of a young group of artists in the direction of destroying traditional canons for the various arts. Its main tenets were directed toward taking rationality from the laws of art and morality. The central nihilism in the movement appeals to the modern existentialist who will destroy organized standards to free the individual for his own aesthetic and moral existence.

DEATH   The terminal point for an existence of alienation, despair, and agony, from an existential point of view. DEATH IS destroyer and preserver. Death will terminate individual existence, but, because the existentialist chooses his own death and accepts its movement toward him over time, he is able to incorporate death as a part of his own existence.

DEHUMANIZATION   This term, to the existentialist, does not refer to a reversion to the primitive, or to the animal-like state. The existentialist views dehumanization to be the state of divesting one's self of all the qualities which have been said to constitute the nature of "man"—of every man. The essentialist, viewing the existentialist, uses the term "dehumanization" in the sense of seeing the existentialist as having reached the condition where he is little more than bestial. Thus, for the essentialist, "humanization" refers to a pleasant process, where to be human is to be in a gratifying condition. For the existentialist, "dehumanization" also implies the condition of having freed one's self from a collective and essentially negative society of man and nature.

DESPAIR   A phase of existential living. To be free, an existential-ist divorces himself from outside knowledge he must admit to, in all logic. He despairs because he must make a continual series of choices, which series can terminate only when he dies. These choices, ironically, bind himself to others from whom he would remain free. To be conscious of his suffering is to be conscious of theirs: therefore, he despairs.

DREAD   The cruel weight of oppression that the existentialist pays for his freedom. We may fear someone or something; we may be free from or for something. But freedom is about and for nothing. Such is true of dread. To face the world condemned to be free to choose only in one's own creating and judging proc-esses must be countered by a depressing force that signifies an impossible withdrawal—such is dread. Yet, to be conscious of one's dread is to be conscious of freedom—states the existential-ist.

ELECTRA COMPLEX   In its most common meaning, the com-plex pertains to the drive, substantially unconscious, for a girl to be drawn in spirit and/or body to the male parent, while being strongly hostile to the female parent, or mother. The existential-ists use this myth in perverted and distorted forms. In one form, the existentialist uses the complex to indicate a double enslave-ment of the individual. She is destroyed because she can never be free from either love or hate. She is forced to give herself to both parents. In another form, the existentialist has complete freedom if she is an Electra: she destroys two individuals at one time. She possesses one "other" (her father) by love, and she possesses another "other" (her mother) by hate. We have two existential views here. In the first, the girl (Electra) is destroyed not because she is loving or hating, but because she hates or loves someone. The moment she admits "someone" as an external force, or as a direct object, she loses her Being-for-Itself. In the second concept, she is freed because she possesses without being possessed. The first concept is more truly existential.

EMPIRICISM   This is opposed by the existentialist, for empiricism is the philosophical and literary doctrine that all knowledge is gained from experience. This experience, of course, must consist of not only sensation, but also of sense and sensibility. The existentialist must oppose empiricism because he believes that knowledge can be obtained only from the flow of his own mental and emotive processes concerning his own existence.

ENCOUNTER   This term, to an existentialist, does not refer to a conscious or unconscious collision between two objects or people. To the existentialist, "encounter" refers to the following areas: (a) the need to continue suffering and agonizing because one encounters the need to choose or not to choose; (b) the continual pressure of rejecting any access to the examining self by any "other" which might control or swallow up or engulf the self; (c) the need to engage Being-for-Itself in order to avoid being Being-for-the-Other. "Encounter" is that experience which is essential to confirm to the self its unique and free existing self in its own terms. Only through encounter with the force which warns the existentialist that he may be chosen, if he does not choose, can the existentialist continue to choose himself for himself.

EPIC   One of the qualities of literature and life that have been taken over by the existentialist in a "reversal" form. He seizes on the traditional qualities of the epic, inverts them, perverts them, and sets up the anti-hero. He does so in order to gain stature by standing apart from what society most admires.

ESSENCE   That which is the central nature of some thing, idea, person, institution, or event. Essence is that which makes one thing—such as a door, a door—that thing and not another thing for that time and place. The very concept of "essence" is that of an invariable nature. The individual obtains his very flavor from the essence of the concept of "man."

ESSENTIALISM The philosophical and literary doctrine that there are objective standards which characterize the class and which, as a result, bind the individuals within the class. There is a commensurable order which determines natural and human phenomena, and does so apart from the single individual. Each man is determined by the essentialism inherent in the personality of man overall, for example.

EXISTENTIALISM That literary philosophy which places its entire emphasis on the individual's existence, an existence which postulates man as free from any natural or human standards in terms of which he must act. The existentialist creates his world of experience through a choice of alternatives, a choice which makes him free from all other men but a choice which enslaves him to his own doubts, uncertainties, and to the consequences of his own choices. He has a consciousness which must consider what his choice has done to others.

EXISTENTIAL HERO A term reserved for the individual who has stood outside society and who has forced society to react to him on his own terms, not on society's.

FAITH This is objected to by the non-Christian existentialist because there is always faith that something will happen, or there is always faith in something. The true existentialist must deny faith because all things, ideas, events, and people have their existence only insofar as his choosing and willing bring them into being as part of the flow of experience. Yet, the existentialist has his own brand of faith. He uses the term "good faith." A man is in "good faith" when he chooses because he ought to choose or ought to choose not to choose; he is in "bad faith" when he chooses what he "ought" to choose and when he chooses what someone wants him to choose.

FOR-ITSELF   An existential term which stresses that each true man must choose, must will, must suffer, and must agonize. He does not choose something, but merely chooses. His merit is in the acts of choosing and willing.

FREEDOM   In existential parlance, that state which results from one's choosing himself. In choosing one's self, one sets himself apart from all other individuals, all other beliefs, all other opinions, and all laws. In being free from traditional standards, which are essential, he is free for deciding, willing, and choosing. A man is free when he chooses his own will over the claims of others and when he accepts the fact of his own death.

HEBRAISM   The literary and ethical philosophy that a stern conscience, an upright heart, a strong collective worship, and the subjection of the intellect to the spirit are basic qualities for the good, the useful, and the religious life.

HELLENISM   The literary and ethical philosophy that the mind, body, and spirit must work in harmony in right thinking, right feeling, and right sensing. This philosophy stresses a strong bent for the spontaneous response to life. Both Hebraism and Hellenism are unacceptable to the existentialist for both, while differing markedly from each other, address themselves to traditional creeds, theses, and dogma.

HUMANISM   The philosophy that experience is designed mainly for training the intellect of man. Interest is in man for certain ideas about the nature of man. Because the philosophy is man-centered and not "a" man-centered philosophy, the intense rationality of humanism is repellent to the existentialist.

IMAGINATION   For the existentialist, that active faculty which changes all experience to a flow of consciousness. The existentialist strives to be conscious of the image of a concrete experience. He rejects the consciousness which presents the image. He must make this rejection because he would be faced with explaining what the image was of. Then he would have to go to external reality for the answer. Being conscious of the image and thing at the same time, he is able to keep reality and its representation all in his own conscious flow of knowledge.

IMMATERIALISM   The philosophy which stresses the mental and emotive phenomena, instead of the world of physical phenomena. This philosophy embraces ideas and emotions about qualities and attributes of real things.

IRRATIONALISM   The philosophy and psychology which look to man's emotive nature and to his subconscious experience. In this philosophy the greatest truths are not organized intellectually but come through intuition. The existentialist is primarily interested in this philosophy, but uniquely so. His irrationalism comes through his insistence that consciousness and subconscious experience must seek the truth of existence, while rejecting the chimera of fixed external truths in science, religion, and ethics.

LIFE   For the existentialist, this is a matter of existing. Existing is a matter of consciousness of choosing, willing, despairing, and suffering. Suffering and despairing are signs and badges of being free. Life is absurd because one must be born into life, and he must die through life. Any man's life is absurd because he must fail. He must fail because he must die. Life is absurd because man has to choose and accept the fact of his death before he can be free in life. Although each freely acting individual gives his own life its own meaning, this meaning is absurd because there can be no meaning derived from life that is not linked with the inevitability of death.

LYING   For the existentialist, this comes about from bad faith. The process of lying is that outward assertion or choice which is different in any degree from the inward choosing, a conscious choosing. Lying is fatal for the existentialist because he must despair over the lie while losing the freedom which he has been given at the cost or price of despair.

MATERIALISM   That philosophy which stresses the primacy of physical nature and which tends to regard man as no more than a form of matter. In this philosophy man is seen as deluding himself through ascribing superior merits to himself as distinct from merits of other physical phenomena. The existentialist is a bitter foe of materialism, as can be seen through the existential thesis that asserts uniqueness in existence.

NARCISSISM   The sexual pleasure obtained from worshiping one's own physical beauty or from admiring one's intellectual gifts. This trait is seen as distinctly non-existential. The existentialist is so seized with despair, alienation, and loneliness through being compelled to be free to know the absurdity of life that narcissim is remote from him. Sadism and masochism are his more likely choices.

NATURALISM   A grim essentialistic philosophy which asserts that life is no more than the chance combination of molecules which are in constant motion. Man uses his intellect to deceive himself as to his being more than an ordinary form of life. Naturalism offers no hope for another existence on a supernatural level. The existentialist really came into being in revolt against naturalism. He is willing to pay the terrible price of isolating himself from his society in order to gain the consciousness of himself as existing in terms of himself.

NATURE   A term which has been poorly used. On one hand, "nature" refers to the central core of meaning in any human or non-human phenomenon. On the other hand, "nature" refers to the world of physical phenomena in both an interpretive and non-interpretive way. The existentialist is exceedingly chary of being pinned down to the reality of the externally-ordered universe of air, sea, and land. There is the nature of the mind, the body, and the spirit. The existential interest in nature extends little farther than the nature of existence as absurd and absurd in terms of the existential individual.

NOTHINGNESS   For the existentialist, this is the very absence of what is, being. Were dread and choice to cancel each other out, there would be no existence. Such a state can take place only in case of insanity or death. Since life is absurd, the onward choosing of the individual is always, through time, toward death, which must be nothingness. Since death is accepted as an integral part of the living experience of an existentialist, nothingness, or no being at all, is woven into the fabric of all consciousness.

"OEDIPUS COMPLEX"   The unresolved drive of the child for the love—through sexual expression—of the opposite parent. In this complex, the pull is in the line (son—mother). Again, the same position would be taken by the existentialist in this complex as was true for the "Electra Complex." Lack of resolution or lack of expression is alien to the existential position. Thus, if the existentialist deals with such literary and psychological complexes, he inverts them. The reader is referred to Highet's *The Classical Tradition* for such literary examples of inversion of the myths.

OTHER (THE)   A term unique to the existential mind. The term is subtle, yet necessary. How does the existentialist handle phenomena such as human and non-human objects? He insists that he, with his consciousness alone, can determine the properties of the objects of his thinking, sensing, and feeling. The society of people and things he must be conscious of because of his choosing and engaging in experience are "the other." His consciousness is a matter of "images of them." If he is just conscious of the images without also being conscious of "them," he is possessed by that which he has as an image. He is no longer free. The existentialist is most sensitive to being loved by anyone and to being conscious of being loved. He wishes to be free from being possessed: he can choose only on his own terms.

RATIONALISM   That philosophy which stresses the primacy of the intellect. While granting the claims of the world of the senses and the world of the emotions, the rationalist gives marked preference to conceptual knowledge.

REALISM   That method which makes concrete the materials of romanticism, classicism, naturalism, and rationalism. Note that in this treatment realism is not regarded as a literary philosophy. The fact that the existentialist must use the realism concretely for the details of the sensory world, the intellectual world, and the emotive world, however much he would invert them, indicates that the existentialist has a problem in that he must use the same method, language-wise, in making his detail specific as that used by essentialists.

ROMANTICISM   That philosophy which stresses the primacy of the heart, the emotions, and the volitions. While granting the claims of those supporting the world of senses and the world of reason, the romanticist gives overwhelming support to the imagination as nearly divine.

SELF-EXAMINATION   For the existentialist this carries more than one meaning, although each meaning is closely related to crisis. We distinguish, of course, "conflict" and "crisis." "Conflict" requires an objective external force or person. "Crisis" is the conscious thought or feeling the existentialist has when he faces a problem that must be seen, judged, and handled within himself and to himself, and by himself. Having faced the agonizing in an existing that demands continual choices which, in each instance, result in repudiating all external force, the existential individual responds to these nearly infinite sets of crises resulting from the nearly infinite sets of alienating choices by a self-examination. This self-examination is made by the individual with no recourse to any other self, and with no other recourse than to the material of his own consciousness. He must, within himself, examine the flow of his own mind, a mind, which in its sensations, sense, and sensibilities can only reveal any experience in terms of a flow which can only reveal that alienated self to the same examining self. Of course, existentialism, as a philosophy, flounders when faced with explaining how the examiner can be the examined, at one and the same time.

SENSIBILITY   A term used to indicate reliance on the emotions. "Sense" refers to the intellect, and "sensation" to the worlds of touch, taste, smell, vision, and sound.

SOCIOCENTRISM   The view that the world is social—group centered. Social interrelationships become important for their own sakes, and the individual finds himself subjected to the state. Both Nazism and Fascism were essentially examples of sociocentrism. The existentialist opposes the philosophy because of his well-taken fear of being crushed, as an individual, by the impersonal power of the state.

SUBJECTIVITY   From the essentialistic point of view this is the thesis that the individual is conscious of the nature and demands of objective phenomena and their criteria, but elects to forego his rational approach in order to make emotive judgments in terms of his own attitudes. From the existential point of view subjectivity is that useful, necessary, and imperative approach to life which rests on an admission and on a claim. The admission is that every subject, even an existentialist, must be an object to others. The claim is that each individual in his choosing, engaging, and willing, holds all experience as both object and image in his consciousness. That is, he is conscious of the image of the object. Thus, each individual, as subjective, cannot escape the subjectivity of his own consciousness, even though he would make such an effort.

TIME   For the existentialist, this is the measure of the flow of consciousness. Each experience bites big chunks out of the approaching future moments which quickly become "presents" and "pasts." While time separates past choices from choices yet to come and while the consciousness of past despairing promises a continuum of despair into future moments, there is a sense in which time is completely unified as a flowing stream. Life flows away with each passing experience, yet life unrolls in the terms of experiences yet to come. While time makes man measure himself in the light of separate encounters, time also presents a movement of death toward the individual. The common element here is that time must make this movement toward the individual, and the individual has agreed to accept the fact of his death, and his acceptance is carried into time by the individual—the existentialist.

Bibliography

General

Allen, E., *Existentialism from Within,* New York, Macmillan, 1953.

Barrett, W., *What Is Existentialism?* New York, Grove Press, 1964.

Blackham, H., *Six Existentialist Thinkers,* New York, Harper Torchbooks, 1959.

Desan, W., *The Tragic Finale,* New York, Harper Torchbooks, 1960.

Grey, J. G., "Idea of Death in Existentialism," *Journal of Philosophy,* 1951, 49, pp. 111–127.

Heidegger, M., *Existence and Being,* Chicago, Regnery, 1949.

——— *The Question of Being,* New York, Twayne, 1958.

Heinemann, F., *Existentialism and the Modern Predicament,* New York, Harper Torchbooks, 1958.

Hintikka, K., "Cogito ergo sum: Inference or Performance," *Philosophical Review,* 1962, 71, pp. 3–32.

——— "Existential Presuppositions and Existential Commitments," *Journal of Philosophy,* 1959, 56, pp. 125–137.

Loose, J., "Christian as Camus's Absurd Man," *Journal of Religion,* 42, pp. 203–214.

Marcel, G., *Being and Having* (tr.), G. Fraser, London, The Harvill Press, 1952.

——— *Men Against Humanity* (tr.), G. Fraser, London, The Harvill Press, 1952.

——— *The Philosophy of Existence,* London, The Harvill Press, 1948.

Maritain, J., *Existence and the Existent,* Garden City, Doubleday and Co., 1960.

Michalson, C., "Existence Is a Mysticism," *Theology Today,* 1955, 12, pp. 155–168.

Murdoch, Iris, *Sartre: Romantic Rationalist,* New Haven, Yale University Press, 1953.

Niebuhr, R., "Dread and Joyfulness: The View of Man as an Affectional Being," *Religion in Life,* 1962, 31, pp. 443–464.

Reinhardt, K., *The Existential Revolt,* Milwaukee, Bruce, 1952.

Roberts, D., *Existentialism and Religious Belief,* Oxford University Press, New York, 1957.

Sartre, Jean-Paul, *Being and Nothingness,* (tr.), Hazel Barnes, Philosophical Library, New York, 1956.

Thompson, J., "Existentialism and Humanism," *Hibbert Journal,* 1949, 170.

Tillich, P., *The Courage to Be,* New Haven, Yale University Press, 1959.

—— "Existential Philosophy," *Journal of the History of Ideas,* 1944, 5, pp. 44–70.

—— "Martin Buber and Christian Thought: His Three-Fold Contribution to Protestantism," *Commentary,* 1948, 5, pp. 515–521.

Wahl, J., *A Short History of Existentialism* (tr.), Williams and S. Maron, New York, Philosophical Library, 1949.

Winn, R., *A Concise Dictionary of Existentialism,* New York, Philosophical Library, 1960.

Psychological Aspects of Existentialism

Arendt, *The Human Condition,* Chicago, University of Chicago Press, 1958.

Boss, M., *The Analysis of Dreams,* New York, Philosophical Library, 1958.

—— *A Daseinsanalytic Approach to the Psychopathology of the*

Phenomenon of Love, New York, Grune and Stratton, 1949.

———— *Psychoanalysis and Daseinsanalysis,* New York, Basic Books, 1963.

Buber, M., *I and Thou,* New York, Scribner's, 1958.

Collins, J., *The Existentialists,* Chicago, Regnery, 1952.

De Beauvoir, S., *The Second Sex,* New York, Knopf, 1953.

De Laurot, E., "Toward a Theory of Dynamic Realism," *Film Culture,* 1955, 1, pp. 2–14.

Frankl, V., *From Death-Camp to Existentialism,* Boston, Beacon Press, 1959.

———— *The Doctor and the Soul,* New York, Knopf, 1957.

Fromm, E., *Psychoanalysis and Religion,* New Haven, Yale, 1950.

———— *Man for Himself,* New York, Rinehart, 1947.

Horney, K., *New Ways in Psychoanalysis,* New York, Norton, 1939.

Jaspers, K., *Existentialism and Humanism,* New York, Moore, 1952.

Kuhn, H., *Encounter with Nothingness,* Chicago, Regnery, 1949.

Laing, R., *The Divided Self,* London, Tavistock, 1960.

May, R., *The Meaning of Anxiety,* New York, Ronald, 1950.

May, R., *Man's Search for Himself,* New York, Norton, 1953.

Papluskas-Ramunas, "Four Modern Philosophies," Lecture Content, Philosophy of Education, University of Ottawa, 1952.

Sartre, J. P., *The Psychology of Imagination,* New York, Philosophical Library, 1948.

———— *Anti-Semite and Jew,* New York, Schocken, 1948.

———— *Existential Psychoanalysis,* New York, Philosophical Library, 1953.

Sonneman, U., *Existence and Therapy,* New York, Grune and Stratton, 1954.

Stern, A., *Sartre: His Philosophy and Psychoanalysis,* New York, Liberal Arts Press, 1953.

Van Den Berg, J., *The Phenomenological Approach to Psychiatry,* Springfield, Mass., Thomas, 1955.

―――― "The Handshake," *Philosophy Today*, 1959, 3 and 4, pp. 28–34.

Weigert, E., "Existentialism and Its Relations to Psychotherapy," *Psychiatry*, 1949, 12, pp. 399–412.

Wild, J., *The Challenge of Existentialism*, Bloomington, Indiana University Press, 1955.

Wolff, W., *Values and Personality*, New York, Grune and Stratton, 1950.

General Literary Philosophy

Abel, L., *Metatheatre: A New View of Dramatic Form*, New York, Hill and Wang, 1963.

Allen, W., *The Modern Novel*, New York, Dutton, 1964.

Barnes, H., *The Literature of Possibility*, Lincoln, University of Nebraska, 1959.

Barrett, W., "What Existentialism Offers Modern Man," *Commentary*, 1951, 48, pp. 113–127.

―――― *Irrational Man: A Study in Existential Philosophy*, New York, Doubleday, 1958.

Beck, M., "Existentialism Versus Naturalism and Idealism," *South Atlantic Quarterly*, 1948, 47, pp. 157–163.

Belcher, W., editor, *J. D. Salinger and the Critics*, Belmont, Wardsworth, 1962.

Brown, S. M., "Atheistic Existentialism of Jean-Paul Sartre," *Philosophical Review*, 1948, 57, pp. 158–166.

Brustein, R., *The Theater of Revolt*, Boston, Little, Brown Co., 1964.

Bultmann, R., "On the Problem of Demythologizing," *Journal of Religion* (S. M. Ogden, tr.), 1962, 42, pp. 96–102.

Copleston, S. J., *Contemporary Philosophy: Studies of Logical Positivism and Existentialism*, Westminster, Newman, 1960.

Cranston, M., *Jean-Paul Sartre*, New York, Grove, 1962.

Cruickshank, J., *Albert Camus and the Literature of Revolt,* New York, Oxford University Press, 1959.

Durfee, H. A., "Albert Camus and the Ethics of Rebellion," *Journal of Religion,* 1958, 38, pp. 29–45.

Ehrmann, J., "Camus and the Existential Adventure," Yale French Studies, 1960, 25, pp. 93–97.

Esslin, M., *The Theatre of the Absurd,* Garden City, Anchor, 1961.

Fallico, A., *Art and Existentialism,* Englewood Cliffs, Prentice-Hall, 1962.

Friedman, M., *Problematic Rebel,* New York, Random House, 1963.

Gassner, J., *Theater at the Crossroads,* New York, Holt et al., 1960.

Gindin, J., *Postwar British Fiction,* Berkeley, California, 1962.

Glicksberg, C., *The Self in Modern Literature,* University Park, Penn. State University Press, 1963.

Greening, T., "Existential Fiction and the Paradox of Ethics," *Antioch Review,* 1963, 23, pp. 93–107.

Grunwald, H., *Salinger, A Critical and Personal Portrait,* New York, Harper, 1962.

Hanna, Thomas, *The Lyrical Existentialist,* New York, Atheneum, 1962.

Hardre, J., "Sartre's Existentialism and Humanism," *Studies in Philology,* 1952, 49, pp. 534–547.

Harris, B., and Brown, J., *Contemporary Theory,* New York, St. Martin's, 1962.

Hassan, I., *Radical Innocence: Studies in the Contemporary American Novel,* Princeton, Princeton University Press, 1961.

Hendel, W. C., "The Subjective as a Problem," *Philosophical Review,* 1953, 62, pp. 327–354.

Hoffman, F., *The Mortal No: Death in the Modern Imagination,* Princeton, Princeton University Press, 1964.

Hook, S., "Pragmatism and Existentialism," *Antioch Review,* 1959, pp. 151–168.

Hooper, S., ed., *Spiritual Problems in Contemporary Literature,* New York, Harper Torchbooks, 1957.

Ionesco, E., *Notes and Counternotes: Writings on the Theater* (D. Watson, tr.), New York, Grove, 1964.

Jaeger, H., "Heidegger's Existential Philosophy and Modern German Literature," *PMLA,* 1952, 67, pp. 655–683.

Jameson, F., *Sartre: The Origins of a Style,* New Haven, Yale University Press, 1961.

Kaelin, E., *An Existentialist Aesthetic,* Madison, University of Wisconsin Press, 1962.

Kerouac, J., "Essentials of Spontaneous Prose," *Evergreen Review,* 1958, 2, p. 73 et seq.

Kerr, W., *The Theater in Spite of Itself,* New York, Simon and Schuster, 1963.

Killinger, J., *Hemingway and the Dead Gods: A Study in Existentialism,* Lexington, University of Kentucky Press, 1960.

Klein, M., *After Alienation,* New York, The World Publishing Co., 1962.

Kostelanetz, R., ed., *On Contemporary Literature,* New York, Avon, 1964.

Lewis, A., *The Contemporary Theater,* New York, Crown, 1962.

Lewis, W., *Men Without Art,* New York, Russell and Russell, 1964.

McEachran, F., "Literature of Existentialism," *Contemporary Review,* 1963, 203, pp. 257–264.

—— *Existentialism and Modern Literature,* New York, Citadel, 1963.

Moore, H. T., *Contemporary American Novelists,* Carbondale, Southern Illinois University Press, 1964.

Nathanson, M., "Jean-Paul Sartre's Philosophy of Freedom," *Social Research,* 1952, 19, pp. 364–380.

O'Brien, J., *Portrait of Andre Gide,* New York, Knopf, 1953.

Percy, W., "Man on the Train: Three Existential Modes," *Partisan Review*, 1956, 23, pp. 478–494.

Rhein, P., *The Urge to Live*, Chapel Hill, North Carolina, 1964.

Santayana, G., "On Existentialism: An Unpublished Letter," *Partisan Review*, 1958, 25, pp. 632 ff.

Sartre, J. P., *Literary Essays*, New York, Philosophical Library, 1957.

Scott, N. A., "The Broken Center: A Definition of the Crisis of Values in Modern Literature," *Chicago Review*, 1959, p. 8.

Thody, P., *Albert Camus: A Study of His Work*, New York, Grove, 1957.

Votow, A., "Literature of Extreme Situations," *Horizon*, 1949, 20, pp. 150–153.

Weatherhead, A., *A Reading of Henry Green*, Seattle, University of Washington Press, 1961.

Weber, Eugene, *Paths to the Present: Aspects of European Thought from Romanticism to Existentialism*, New York, Dodd, Mead, 1960.

Wellwarth, G., *The Theater of Protest and Paradox*, New York, New York University Press, 1964.

Wilson, C., *Religion and the Rebel*, London, Gallancz, 1957.

The Literary Scene: Naturalism, Romanticism, and Existentialism

Adams, R., "Romanticism and the American Renaissance," *American Literature*, 1951, 23, pp. 419–432.

Allen, E., *Existentialism from Within*, New York, Macmillan, 1953.

Barrett, W., "American Fiction and American Values," *Partisan Review*, 1951, 18, pp. 681–690.

Current-Garcia and Patrick, *Realism and Romanticism in Fiction*, Chicago, Scott-Foresman, 1962.

McKillop, A., *The Early Masters of English Fiction,* Lawrence, University of Kansas Press, 1956.

Orians, G., "The Rise of Romanticism, 1805–1855," *Transition in American Literary History* (H. Clark, ed.), Durham, Duke University Press, 1953.

Stewart, R., "Dreiser and the Naturalistic Heresy," *Virginia Quarterly Review,* 1958, 34, pp. 100–116.

Walcutt, C., *American Literary Naturalism,* Minneapolis, Minnesota University Press, 1956.

Weber, E., *Paths to the Present,* New York, Dodd Mead, 1960.

Early Existential Notes in Literature

INTRODUCTORY REMARKS AND BIBLICAL NOTES

Michalson, C., "Existentialism Is a Mysticism," *Theology Today,* 1955, 12, pp. 155–168.

Roberts, D., *Existentialism and Religious Belief,* New York, Oxford University Press, 1957.

Tillich, P., "Martin Buber and Christian Thought," *Commentary,* 1948, 5, pp. 515–521.

THE RENAISSANCE STREAM

Bennett, J., "An Aspect of the Evolution of Seventeenth Century Prose," *Review of English Studies,* 17, 1941, pp. 281–297.

Carter, C., *The English Church in the Seventeenth Century,* Longmans, Green and Co., 1909.

Highet, G., *The Classical Tradition,* New York, Oxford University Press, Galaxy, 763 pp.

Spurgeon, C., *Mysticism in English Literature,* Cambridge University Press, 1913.

THE AUGUSTAN AGE

Bate, W., *From Classic to Romantic,* Cambridge, Harvard University Press, 1949.

Churchill, R., *English Literature of the Eighteenth Century,* London University Tutorial Press, 1953.

Hipple, W., *The Beautiful, the Sublime, and the Picturesque in Eighteenth Century British Aesthetic Theory,* Carbondale, Southern Illinois University Press, 1957.

Humphreys, A., *The Augustan World: Society, Thought and Letters in Eighteenth-Century England,* New York, 1954, Harper Torchbooks.

Thompson, J., "Existentialism and Humanism," *Hibbert Journal,* 1949, pp. 170 ff.

PRE-ROMANTIC LITERATURE PERIOD

Babbitt, I., *Rousseau and Romanticism,* Boston, Houghton Mifflin Co., 1919.

Beers, H., *A History of English Romanticism in the Eighteenth Century,* New York, Holt, 1898.

Hatzfield, H., "A Clarification of the Baroque Problem in the Romance Literatures," *Comparative Literature,* I, 1949, pp. 113–139.

Morgues, O., *Metaphysical, Baroque, and Precieux Poetry,* Oxford, Oxford University Press.

ROMANTIC LITERATURE PERIOD

Abrams, M., *The Mirror and the Lamp: Romantic Theory and the Critical Tradition,* New York, Oxford University Press, 1953.

Bowra, C., *The Romantic Imagination,* New York, Oxford University Press, 1961 (Galaxy).

Davis, J., *Discussions of William Wordsworth,* Boston, Heath, 1964.

Kaufman, P., "Defining Romanticism: A Survey and a Program," *M.L.A. Notes,* XL, 1925, pp. 193–204.

Railo, E., *The Haunted Castle,* London, Routledge, 1927.

VICTORIAN LITERATURE PERIOD

Baudelaire, C., *The Mirror of Art,* Doubleday, Anchor, 1956.

Buckley, J., *The Victorian Temper,* Cambridge, Harvard University Press, 1951.

Cecil, Lord D., *Victorian Novelists,* Chicago, University of Chicago Press, 1958.

Cruse, A., *The Victorians and Their Reading,* Boston, Houghton Mifflin, 1935.

Praz, Mario, *The Hero in Eclipse in Victorian Fiction,* London, Oxford University Press, 1956.

GEORGIAN LITERATURE PERIOD

Braybrooke, P., *Some Victorian and Georgian Catholics,* London, Burns, Oates, and Washbourne, Ltd., 1932.

Elwin, M., *Old Gods Falling,* New York, Macmillan, 1939.

Muir, E., *Essays on Contemporary Literature,* New York, Viking, 1926.

Priestley, J., *Figures in Modern Literature,* Dodd, Mead and Co., 1924.

Swinnerton, F., *The Georgian Scene: A Literary Panorama,* New York, Farrar and Rinehart, 1934.

CONTINENTAL EUROPE LITERARY SCENE

Bennett, J., *Baudelaire,* Princeton, Princeton University Press, 1944.

Bentley, E., *The Cult of the Superman,* R. Hale, 1947.

Buchanan, R., *The Fleshy School of Poetry,* Strahan and Co., 1872.

Davis, H., *Tolstoy and Nietzsche,* New York, New Republic, 1929.

Fayer, M., *Gide, Freedom and Dostoevsky,* Lane Press, 1946.

Garrod, H., *Tolstoi's Theory of Art,* London, The Clarendon Press, 1935.

Hromadka, J., *Doom and Resurrection,* Madrus House, 1945.

Huneker, J., *Egoists: A Book of Supermen,* New York, Scribner's Sons, 1909.

Kaufmann, W., *Nietzsche,* Princeton, Princeton University Press, 1950.

Kvito, D., *A Philosophical Study of Tolstoy,* New York, Columbia University Press, 1927.

Olivero, F., *Rilke: A Study in Poetry and Mysticism,* London, Heffer, Ltd., 1931.

Sargeaunt, G., *The Classical Spirit,* The Cloanthus Press, 1936.

MODERN EXISTENTIAL WRITERS
France

Ayer, A. J., "Novelist–Philosophers," *Horizon,* March, 1946.

Clark, E., "The World of Jean Genet," *Partisan Review,* XVI, 1949, pp. 442–448.

Coe, R., *Eugene Ionesco,* New York, Grove, 1961.

Fowlie, W., *Dionysus in Paris,* New York, Meridiana, 1960.

Fucciani, F., "Genet and the Maids," *Tulane Drama Review,* VII, 1963, pp. 42–59.

Grossvogel, D., *The Selfconscious Stage in Modern French Drama,* New York, Columbia University Press, 1958.

Guicharnaud, J., *Modern French Theater from Giraudoux to Beckett,* New Haven, Connecticut, Yale University Press, 1961.

────── and Beckelman, *Modern French Theater,* New Haven, Yale University Press, 1961.

Jacottet, P., "Note a propos de Jean Tradieu," *Nouvelle Revue Francaise,* July, 1960.

Jean Genet, "A Note on Theater," (Frechtman, tr.), *Tulane Drama Review,* Spring, 1963.

John, S., "Image and Symbol in Albert Camus," *French Studies,* 1955, pp. 42–53.

────── "Obsession and Technique in the Plays of Jean Anouilh," *French Studies,* 11, 1957.

Lesage, L., *"Jean Giraudoux, His Life and His Works,* University Park, Pennsylvania State University Press, 1959.

────── "Jean Giraudoux, Surrealism, and the German Romantic Ideal," *Illinois Studies in Language and Literature,* 36, 1952.

Nelson, B., "The Balcony and Parisian Existentialism," *Tulane Drama Review,* VII, 1963, pp. 60–79.

Pronko, L., *Avant Garde: The Experimental Theater in France,* Berkeley, University of California Press, 1962.

Reck, R., "Malraux's Heroes: Activists and Aesthetes," *The University of Kansas City Review,* 27, 1961.

Roth, L., "Albert Camus," *Philosophy,* October, 1955, pp. 291–303.

Sartre, J. P., *Saint Genet: Comedien et Martyr,* Paris, Gallimard, 1952.

Wellwarth, G., *The Theater of Protest and Paradox,* New York, New York University Press, 1964.

ROUMANIA

Coe, R., *Eugene Ionesco,* New York, Grove, 1961.

Doubrovsky, J., "Ionesco amd the Comic of Absurdity," *Yale French Studies,* 23, 1959, pp. 3–10.

Knowles, D., "Ionesco and the Mechanisms of Language," *Modern Drama,* V, 1962, pp. 7–10.

Watson, D., "The Plays of Ionesco," *Tulane Drama Review,* III, i, 1958, pp. 48–53.

GERMANY

Davian, D., "Justice in the Works of Friedrich Durrenmatt," *Kentucky Foreign Language Quarterly,* 9, 1962, pp. 181–193.

Klarmann, A., "Friedrich Durrenmatt and the Tragic Sense of Comedy," *Tulane Drama Review,* IV, 1960, pp. 77–104.

Peppard, M., "The Grotesque in Durrenmatt's Dramas," *Kentucky Foreign Language Quarterly,* II, 1962, pp. 36–44.

Seidmann, P., "Modern Swiss Drama: Frisch and Durrenmatt," *Books Abroad,* 34, 1960, pp. 112–114.

Waidson, H., "Durrenmatt: The Comedy of Despair," *Nation,* CXC, 1960, pp. 34–35.

Ziolkowski, T., "Max Frisch: Moralist Without a Moral," *Yale French Studies,* 29, 1962, pp. 132–141.

SPAIN

Cruma in Premi Joan Santamaria, 1957, Barcelona, Editorial Nerida, 1958.

Morrissett, A., "Dialogue with Arrabal," New York, *Evergreen Review*, 15, 1960.

BELGIUM

Abel, L., "Our Man in the Sixteenth Century: Michel de Ghelerode," *Tulane Drama Review*, 8, 1963, pp. 62–71.

Draper, S., "An Interview with Michel de Ghelerode," *Tulane Drama Review*, VIII, i, 1963, pp. 39–50.

Grossvogel, D., "The Flight of the Comic Author and Some New Departures in Contemporary Comedy," *Romantic Review*, XLV, 1954, pp. 268–270.

ENGLAND

Allen, W., "Evelyn Waugh, and Graham Greene," *Irish Monthly*, LXXVII, 1949, X, pp. 16–22.

Amis, K., "Psyche of the Future," *Mlle*, 54: 40–1, Jan. 62.

―――― *New Maps of Hell, A Survey of Science Fiction*, New York, Harcourt, Brace and Co., 1960.

Cohn, R., "The World of Harold Pinter," *Tulane Drama Review*, VI, iii, 1962, pp. 55–68.

―――― *Samuel Beckett: The Comic Gamut*, New Brunswick, Rutgers University Press, 1962.

Cottrell, B., "Second Time Charms: The Theater of Graham Greene," *Modern Fiction Studies*, III, Autumn, 1957, pp. 249–255.

Deming, B., "John Osborne's War Against the Philistines," *Hudson Review*, XI, 1959, pp. 411 and 419.

DeVitis, A., *Graham Greene*, New York, Grosset and Dunlap, 1964.

Esslin, M., "Pinter and the Absurd," *Twentieth Century*, CLXIX, 1961, pp. 176–185.

Fergusson, F., *The Human Image in Dramatic Literature*, Garden City, Doubleday, 1957.

Hall, J., "The Fiction of Henry Green: Paradoxes of Pleasure-and-Pain," *Kenyon Review*, 19, 1957, pp. 76–88.

Kettle, A., *An Introduction to the English Novel,* London, Hutchinson's, 1951, 1953.

Leavis, F., *Two Cultures? The Significance of C. P. Snow,* London, Chatto and Windus, 1962.

Marowitz, "Oh Mother Is It Worth It?" *Theatre Arts,* 46, xi, 1962, pp. 26–27.

O'Faolain, S., "Graham Greene: I Suffer; Therefore, I Am," *The Vanishing Hero: Studies in Novelists of the Forties,* London, Eyre and Spottiswoode, 1956.

Popkin, H., "Williams, Osborne, or Beckett?" *New York Times Book Review,* November 18, 1960, pp. 32–33, 119–121.

Taylor, J., *Anger and After,* London, Methuen & Co., Ltd., 1962.

Tindall, W., *Forces in Modern British Literature,* New York, Vintage, 1956.

Trilling, O., "The Young British Dramatists," *Modern Drama,* III, 1960, pp. 168–177.

Wain, J., "Great Burroughs Affair," *New Republic,* 147, December, 1962, pp. 21–23.

Wann, C., "There's No Place on Earth Like the World," *Theatre Arts,* 46, xi, 1962, pp. 26–27.

Weatherhead, A., *A Reading of Henry Greene,* Seattle, University of Washington Press, 1964.

AMERICAN CONTEMPORARY SCENE

Balakian, N., *The Creative Present: Notes on Contemporary American Fiction,* New York, Doubleday, 1964.

Barr, D., "Saints, Pilgrims, and Artists," *Commonweal,* 67, Oct. 25, 1957.

Bellow, S., *The Living Novel* (Granville Hicks, ed.), New York, Macmillan, 1957.

Costello, D., "The Language of *The Catcher in the Rye,*" *American Speech,* October, 1959.

Ellison, R., "Change the Joke and Slip the Yoke," *Partisan Review,* Spring, 1958, p. 218.

Fiedler, L., *Love and Death in the American Novel,* New York, Criterion Books, 1960.

Frye, N., *The Anatomy of Criticizing,* Princeton, Princeton University Press, 1957.

Giraud, R., *The Unheroic Hero,* New Brunswick, Rutgers University Press, 1957.

Gold, H. (ed.), *Fiction of the Fifties,* New York, 1959.

—— "The Mystery of Personality in the Novel," *The Living Novel,* New York, 1957.

—— "A Dog in Brooklyn," "A Girl in Detroit," "A Life Among the Humanities," *Man and His Measure* (Connolly, ed.), New York, Harcourt, 1964.

Hassan, I., *Radical Innocence: Studies in the Contemporary American Novel,* Princeton, Princeton University Press, 1961.

Hicks, G., "J. D. Salinger: Search for Wisdom," *Saturday Review,* July 25, 1959.

Horton, R., and Edwards, W., *Backgrounds of American Literary Thought,* New York, Appleton Century Crofts, Inc., 1952.

Kerouac, J., "The Origins of the Beat Generation," *Playboy,* VI, June, 1959.

Klein, M., *After Alienation,* New York, World Publishing Co., 1962.

Kostelanetz, R., *On Contemporary Literature,* New York, Avon, 1964.

Mailer, N., "Our Country and Our Culture," *Partisan Review,* May–June, 1952.

Moore, H., *Contemporary American Novelists,* Carbondale, Southern Illinois University Press, 1964.

Rovit, E., "Bernard Malamud and the Jewish Literary Tradition," *Critique,* Winter–Spring, 1960.

Stern, R., "Hip Hell, and the Navigator: An Interview with Norman Mailer," *Western Review,* Winter, 1959.

—— "Henderson's Bellow," *The Kenyon Review,* XXI, Autumn, 1959, pp. 659–660.

Tallman, W., "Kerouac's Sound," *Evergreen Review,* IV, 11, p. 187.

Waldmeir, J., *Recent American Fiction: Some Critical Views,* Boston, Houghton Mifflin, 1963.

Zimbardo, R., "Symbolism and Naturalism in Edward Albee's *The Zoo Story,*" *Twentieth Century Literature,* VIII, 1960.

INDEX